All Scripture references taken from the KJV of the Bible, unless otherwise indicated.

Freshwater Press USA

Don't Refuse Me, Lord (Book 1 of 4)

Series titles: **Don't Refuse Me, Lord** (Book 1)

Lord, Help My Debt (Book 2)

As My Soul Prospers (Book 3)

Don't Work for Money (Book 4)

ISBN: 978-1-893555-75-4

Table of Contents

Don't Refuse Me, Lord

Freshwater

Freshwater Press, USA

Don't Refuse Me, Lord

A vacationing couple went out to the ocean. To enjoy the view better, they climbed to a high place that overlooked miles and miles of deep, blue water, an ideal place to meet up with the presence of God. But once atop this overlook, the woman told the man that she wanted to play a game. Although they had been married many years, (or because of it), the woman had devised a plan to do harm to her husband. Because she lied convincingly, he allowed her to tie his hands behind his back with a zip tie. Thinking this was all in fun, he went along, never suspecting foul play.

Immediately after binding his hands as tightly as she could, she walked away from him, as though going back to their hotel. Just as he turned to follow her, she turned again and began running very quickly toward him. She reached out both of her free arms. Her intent was to push him over the edge, into that beautiful, but shark-infested ocean.

The man was an athlete, quick and agile. Still thinking this was a game, he stepped aside. She missed him and went flying over the edge of that high place, falling, screaming into the cold ocean. He remembered that she was not a strong swimmer, and his heart went out to her as he heard her gurgled scream for help. She struggled desperately against the choppy, brutal waves. Fear strengthened her call when she saw the dorsal fin of a great white shark. *"Help! Help!* she gurgled as water began to fill her mouth.

"I can't, he yelled, but it was heard only faintly, *"Help!"*

A third, and last time, she yelled, but it was heard only faintly, *"Help!"*

And for the last time, he called to her, *"You've tied my hands."* He wept because he loved her, and wanted so much to help her, but was unable. Being an excellent swimmer, he could have saved her, but his hands were tied. They were quite a distance from the hotel, so there was no one he could call on; there was nothing he could do. Her *free* hands had been devising evil, which backfired on her.

Have you ever needed the Lord in a desperate way? Have you ever needed Him to bless you mightily? Have you ever needed the Lord, with a time or date deadline staring at you? You've called on Him once or twice already; and today is the final day to pay that bill or tell the surgeon, *"No!"*

Loud or faint, depending on your faith, strength and personality, it's your third and desperate cry for help. Why hasn't God responded? Why is God refusing you?

His Hands

It may seem as though you're drowning in your situation, or you're surrounded by the specter of sharks. What is God doing? Is He just standing around with His holy hands behind His holy back?

You may have wondered about God's hands, since we are ever looking to Him, and them. Children know by rote: *"By His hands, we all are fed."* There is so much that comes from His hand: protection, covering, shelter, prosperity, gifts, anointing, and blessings. In our desperate situations we are looking for God, and specifically for His hands, to help and bless us.

Remember daddy's or grandpa's hands treating you to candy or chewing gum? Can you recall a *well done* pat on the head or it's-going-to-be okay hug? Shouldn't God's hands be something like that, doing what you ask, need, or something even better? But why aren't God's hands blessing you, helping you and prospering you? Why aren't God's hands being nice to you and giving you the things you want and need? Are His hands really tied behind His back? Do they seem tied in your situation? I know you've never pushed the Lord over the edge, but have you tied His hands? If they are tied, He can only refuse you.

As the man on the cliff watched his wife, (evil though she was), wrestling with the sea, he would have been a fool to jump in with her and also drown—, even for love. As our merciful and compassionate God watches you in your struggles, He wants to come in and help you; it's one of His attributes. He is our very present Help in times of trouble, (Psalm 46:1). The Lord is our Helper, (Heb 13:6b); but because of your actions, can He help?

How's the Water?

God loves you, but are you in the kind of situation that God can jump in with you? First of all, is the door open for Him to come in? The Scriptures tell us that God opens doors that no man can shut and closes doors that no man can open. The same is true for you. Jesus stands at the door and knocks. He is waiting for you to open the door. You have the power and control over not only the door of Salvation, but also other spiritual doors. Negative spiritual doors are closed for our protection, and you should take care not to open them. What spiritual doors have you opened or closed? Are the conditions favorable for God to visit or come to help you? Is He invited, and will you open the door?

How is the water once He gets there? Is it troubled or calm? Are you secure in who you are, in Him?

Salvation

Are you one of His? Are you saved? Have you accepted Jesus Christ as your Lord and Savior? Salvation opens the door for God to come in; it makes you family. You wouldn't let a stranger in your house, and give them your children's dinner, would you? God has a family--, those who have accepted Him as Lord and Savior, those who have invited Him into their hearts and to be the Lord of their lives. Are you in the family of God? Are you one of those with whom He has relationship?

God talks about children, Sons and Daughters, all through the Bible; this is what is important to Him. If you are not saved, then you are as a stranger. He has good things, good success, help and prosperity set aside for His children--, His sons and daughters. But if you are not one of His, God may have to refuse you.

But Jesus said unto her, Let the children first be filled; for it is not meet to take the children's bread, and cast it unto the dogs (Mark 7:27).

If you are not Saved but are reading this book it is not too late to become Saved and one of His (Acts 2). If you are not Saved, I am not calling you an animal; the above verse means that those who are called the children of God will be given to first, then the others may partake of the leftovers.

> And she answered and said unto Him, *"Yes, Lord: yet the dogs under the table eat of the children's crumbs."* (Mark 7:28)

Relationship

Even if you are Saved, what is your *relationship* with God? Consider your relationship with people and theirs with you. You've got certain relatives and acquaintances who only call or come around when they want or need something. You can count on it. If they are on the other end of the phone, or their fingerprints are on your doorbell, they want money, food, your car, or they have a get rich quick scheme for you.

Do you just call on God when you need something from Him? Yes? This could be why you are reaping the *same kind* of friends and relatives in your life. It could be why He is refusing you. Are those suitable conditions for Him to visit or help you in your situation? Do you give to the call-me-when-you-want-something relative. No. Because having **no**

relationship is not likely to make you go out of your way to help someone. Those conditions are not inviting or acceptable unless you are moved by the Spirit of God or as an act of kindness or ministry.

Who would you even go out of your way to help if mercy or compassion does not drive you to give to them? Those with whom you have relationship. Even if the face is that of a stranger, if you are Spirit-led, if God told you to do it, then that person is known by the Spirit, and that is still based on relationship--, yours with God and your obedience to God's voice.

The children of God are fed first and fed to satisfaction. The children of faith are supposed to be so abundantly cared for that their leftovers may feed the unsaved. That is what the principle of gleaning was all about in the Old Testament, (Ruth 2:2-23). The well off, the prosperous, those with abundant harvests were to leave the corners of the fields for the poor, the underprivileged, the homeless and the downtrodden. Those people could come themselves and reap from a field. The poor did not have to be embarrassed while receiving handouts. They actually worked for what they harvested, although they may not have had a field to plant or cultivate. Gleaning was still working; they worked for their supper. The hungry in that day could hold up a sign, *Hungry, will glean for food*.

Can you see how our modern-day welfare system is not spiritually correct? That's why it doesn't work. Gleaning promotes dignity and self-respect because the man who gleans works, gets food and seed. Handouts of food and necessary, *now* things do not include seed. And we all know that being seedless leads to laziness and despair. And laziness leads to corruption. As one of *His*, you are able to have a field, plant it, and harvest it. God will help you each step of the way. As one of His, you shouldn't be begging God. You should have enough for yourself, and enough to be a blessing to others who are poor or temporarily without. Spiritually and in the natural, we should be very prosperous. Spiritually we should be so filled with the Word, teachings, messages, Spiritual gifts and Fruits of the Spirit that out of our belly should flow Living Water. We should have a Word in season to assist the flailing or failing Sinner or Saint.

Financially, we should be living in so much prosperity and abundance that the Sinner, who is not supposed to be as successful and prosperous as we are, should come to us as a borrower. We should be set in place to lend. The saved are not supposed to be going to the unsaved for help. We should be going to God. Then when sinners see how well we are doing, they will ask to know more about God. The Sinner should be asking, *Who is their God?* Prosperity can be a great witnessing tool. God will give you prosperity, especially if that's what you you're going to be using it for.

With Salvation comes amenities such as spiritual gifts, grace, favor, and blessings that include being the head only and not the tail, (Deuteronomy 28:13). When we give, it will be given back to us, pressed down, shaken together and running over, (Luke 6:38). The Word says that if we keep this covenant, everything we do should prosper, (Deuteronomy 29:9). We should be in health and prosper as our soul prospers, (3 John 2), and so on, to the tune of several hundred prosperity and success promises God has made to us.

In Salvation we grow from servants to friends, to sons and daughters of God. We are adopted, (Romans 8:15) into the family of God. So when you call on God in faith, being one of His, He moves to help you. He comes to aid you in your need. He comes to bless you, protect you, feed you, and keep you. Whatever you need, He will give it to you; He will not fail his own.

Faith

God responds to faith, not whining, complaining, belly aching, hollering, and slobbering. You say you're praying? Then *say* something. **Pray** something. Yes, pray with emotion and supplication, not just making noises, unless you are so overcome that the Holy Spirit is making utterances that you may not understand. It is best that the noise you make makes some sense to God and the ministering spirits that He has given charge over you. If you just yell or scream at the top of your voice and lungs, perhaps it's a scream of torment indicating the need for deliverance, or that you are in the *process* of deliverance.

God, who is the Ancient of Days, and that's pretty old, may have to inquire of His heavenly host, ***"What did he just say?"***

The Angels might echo what you just yelled, *"Ahhhhhhhhh!"*

God might say, ***"What does that mean? What is, Ahhhhhhhhh? What does he want?***

OK, God knows your heart, God knows your needs. But why send Him a puzzle to have to figure out when you can just say, "God, heal me." *Or*, "God save my child"? And by *saying* it, your own faith increases. You *hear* yourself <u>**say**</u> what you want; faith comes by hearing. What comes by screaming?

Cause God to take action on your behalf by calling Him to His remembrance of His Word. God responds to faith. If you don't have enough faith to *say* what you want, then you don't have enough faith. Faith comes by hearing, so **say** what you want. Then God can hear it and bless you. <u>**Say**</u> it so you can hear it and grow more in faith. Without faith it is impossible to please God, (Hebrews 11:6).

When you are pleased with friends and family, you do good things for them. You make kind gestures toward kind people, don't you? When you are pleased with someone, you bless them or give them time, attention, or gifts. You want something from God? *Then **please Him.*** You can please Him by acting in faith. If you are asking, praying and moving in faith, and God can and will visit you. God will not refuse your faith.

Praise and Worship

God inhabits the praises of His people. If God is in your midst, that's the best time to ask Him for what you want. Praise and worship please God. He will not refuse you.

When my mom comes to visit, it's the best time to ask her to make me an apple pie. How can she refuse when she's staying at my house? When God comes to hear your beautiful words, songs, and acts of worship toward Him, although we should also purely worship and not always be asking for things, still, that's the best time to ask Him for what you want.

Sowing & Reaping

People

God gives seed to the Sower, (Isaiah 51:10). That's you, the Sower. But *where* do you sow those seeds? You sow them in the Earth. *Where*, you may again ask. You don't have a farm. I asked God that question. The answer I received is that spiritual seeds can be sown everywhere in the Earth, in the earthen vessels, you are the Earth. People are the Earth. What we sow in people comes up as a harvest, whether we sow in time, energy, gifts, love, hate or jealousy. It will grow and then reach a time of maturity and harvest.

Water

We can sow in water. A catfish farmer builds a pond and sows catfish in it. Living catfish is used as the seed. Then he waits for them to multiply and grow so he can harvest the mature ones and send them to market. In the next season he doesn't have to restock. Usually they will multiply on their own.

When we go fishing for souls, we sow the Word as bait to reap a harvest of men.

Soil

We can sow into the soil. Churches and ministries are considered good soil for tithes, offerings and other giving. God sows. He sows into man, then teaches men to sow. It started way back in the Garden at Eden and continues every time God gives a blessing, a Word, a promise, pours out anointing and makes a covenant. After He sows into you, He then expects you to pass it on, and thereby blessing others.

Air

We sow into the air. *Air?* you may say. Air. What we say, we sow. Our words are seed. If we say kind things about people, we reap kindness. When we sow evil things, we reap evil.

For he that Soweth to his flesh shall reap of the flesh
reap corruption. But he that soweth to the spirit
shall of the spirit reap life everlasting (Galatians 6:8).

Harvest Time

Since you're going to reap, you need God. And God shows up at harvest time. Whatever you've planted, good or bad, if it's been watered and cultivated, it's going to come up, unless you repent of having planted it in a timely fashion. But, in the case of negative things, sometimes it comes up anyway. It may not be as bad as it could have been because you repented. It may come up, but God's Mercy may cause it to wither on the vine. Or it may come up as less than it was to be because of your repentance. Even if you planted something other than what God gave you to plant, it's still going to come up.

God is not coming to harvest thistles, weeds, and works of the flesh. God refuses to come to harvest that. Most of the time when that kind of harvest is in the devil, the Counterfeiter will gladly come along to facilitate that harvest.

There you are, in the middle of a bad situation, calling on God. *Where is He?* Did you plant the seeds He gave you, or did you plant the seeds that caused a bad situation to manifest? That could be why He's refusing.

The conditions of Salvation, faith, praise and worship, and proper sowing is what God will run to. It's what He will visit. He will not refuse that. He comes with purpose to reap and then give more seed, but He will avoid the works of the flesh. Wouldn't you? You should.

Now the works of the flesh are these adultery, fornication, uncleanness, lasciviousness, idolatry, witchcraft, hatred, variance, emulations, wrath, strife, seditions, heresies, Envyings murder, drunkenness, revelings, and such like. They which do such things shall not inherit the Kingdom of God,

(Galatians 5:19-21)

Help Me, Lord

But what things have you done to help yourself? What have you planted? Whatever you've planted, you've got to harvest it. Gotta. It's the law. Oh, you're in poverty or not in prosperity? How did that happen? Maybe you sowed stinginess or dishonor. Maybe you robbed God. Perhaps you cursed someone's money. Maybe you disrespected your boss's money, gave discounts where there should have been no discounts. Maybe you were unfaithful in someone else's money. Maybe you cursed your own money by not paying tithes and giving offerings. Now it's time to reap. You will reap corruption, and that's the curse.

Poverty is a curse, (Deuteronomy 28).

How did poverty come about in your life? Disobedience? Somebody you're connected to by blood was disobedient. *Was it you?*

Christ's death redeemed us from the curse of the law being made a curse for us, for it is written, cursed is everyone that hangeth on a tree. (Galatians 3:13).

Yes, there is the law. But thank God for Grace. Jesus said that He came that we might have life and have it more abundantly. He has taken the curse for us so we can live in the blessings. That is God's intent that we have abundance, which means more than enough for life and godliness, (2 Peter 1:3), and enough left over to share.

Abundant Children Tithe

There was a woman in the Bible, not being a Jew, who wanted only the crumbs from the table, (Mark 7:28), so her child could be healed. She had enough faith to know who Jesus was, and she knew He had enough for His own. And there will be leftovers for others to glean. She was ready to glean. Abundance is having enough for herself, family, and enough to share, enough to leave or give to gleaners.

The tithe is as much an act of willingness, obedience, and honor as it is an act of giving. It is an act of love for God. It is an act of love toward the people who you believe your tithe-paying will help. You know the lost, the indigent, the ignorant--, those who do not know who God is, and the unsaved. Paying the tithe is act of obedience because you love God.

If you love me, you will obey what I command.

(John 14:15)

Paying the tithe is an act of and reflection of abundance. God will bless you abundantly when you show Him that you are a tither. People with the above-listed characteristics, and others, are the kind of people that impress God. He will prosper you so He can establish covenant with you. We should follow His Word; we should tithe.

More Money

You may be thinking that if you were rich, you could afford to tithe. Rich or not, you can't afford not to tithe. Further, you can afford to tithe because it's a percentage. It's 10%. No matter how much you make, it's still the same amount, in a sense.

As I taught my 10-year-old niece Ashley about the tithe, I asked her if she made $10 per week would she pay her tithe of a dollar. She said, "Yes." I asked her she made $100 per week; would she pay the $10 tithe? She said, "Yes." When asked about receiving $1000 and paying a tithe of $100, she hesitated. Then finally and reluctantly said, "*Yes*." We computed that the tithe on $1,000,000 would be $100,000. She said she didn't think that she could pay that because it was so much money. She was ten years old then.

We are no longer children, but how many adults want to give God the peanuts and keep the cashews? How many want to give God what feels comfortable to them and expect Him to not only just take it, but turn around and bless them some more? And don't even mention any consequences of robbing Him. Pray that you are not like that. If you don't honor Him, He says He will esteem you lightly. Where are the people in your life that you esteem lightly--, don't think much of? Is that where you want to be with God? Of course not.

> Poverty and shame shall be to him that refuseth instruction, but he that regardeth reproof shall be honored.
>
> (Proverbs 13:18)

Is poverty what you're calling on God about? To be honored by God needs to be blessed out of poverty. To adhere to instruction, to follow the Word of God will cause you to receive honor and blessings from God. That is why people believe that ignorance and poverty go together, and they do. Ignorance of the laws of God go with poverty. Having education, knowledge, wisdom, and experience, know-how even in the world should result in a person making more money. The exceptions are the people who work God's spiritual laws. It doesn't matter who or what they are and how they follow the rules of prosperity in the world. If they have put God first, watch them prosper.

Of course it would be much wiser to follow natural and spiritual laws of prosperity, but with God all things are possible. Learn God's laws of money and do them. Tithing is not paying 10% once in a while. It is paying 10% of your increase every time God increases you. Abraham gave a tenth of all, (Genesis 14). If people who tithe have become wealthy, it's because of working the principles of God. If you are prosperous and want to stay prosperous, you should tithe. If you are not yet prosperous, tithing is involved in getting you there. God wants to establish His covenant so He makes us to prosper so He can do just that (Deuteronomy. 8:18).

Oh, as soon as you get a raise on your job or get all your bills paid off, you're going to tithe. If that's what's keeping you and 80% of all professed Christians from tithing, then God could just make all of His people rich right now. Rich people do not automatically tithe either. The more money you make, the greater the dollar amount the tithe will be. If you are struggling with the tithe on $1000 God's not going to trust you with the tithe on $10,000. Even a ten-year-old knew that would be a challenge for her.

If you're struggling with whether or not to pay your credit card, which has a limit of $500, evidenced by erratic late or non-payments to the credit card company, do you think they're going to increase your limit? No. God is much wiser than a bank or lending agency. And He has much better gifts. If you're not being faithful with the spiritual things that you've been given so far, do you think He's going to increase your blessings?

The sane man will answer, *"No!"*

Honor

Tithing comes out of the heart and the soul. It is an act of love and obedience. It reflects your relationship with the Father. It is an act of faith and giving. Tithing is an act of honor. We not only honor God by giving Him His due, but we also honor *ourselves* by behaving responsibly and respectfully and obeying the laws of God. The Word says that if we are willing and obedient, we will eat the good and the fat of the land, (Genesis 45:18). If you are paying your tithes reluctantly and begrudgingly, then you are **obedient** but not willing. If you want to pay your tithes but don't because you are too unorganized or undisciplined, then you are *willing* but not obedient. Either way, if you're not working the principle, the principle won't work for you. You have to be willing <u>and</u> obedient.

You even honor man. When you go to that wedding, birthday party, or 50th anniversary, do you take a gift? The recipient of that gift honors you with fellowship, then later, a thank you note. You honor them and they honor you. It's Biblical.

Think of it as a remembrance. An Angel of the Lord came to tell Cornelius that his giving had come up as a memorial to him (Acts 10:31). Cornelius was an officer in the Italian army; he wasn't even saved. So as Cornelius had honored God in his giving and prayers, God could then honor Cornelius.

Think of all the people who gave your baby a shower gift or you a housewarming gift when you moved into your new house. Don't you remember them fondly? That's a memorial. When or if they need something, they can probably count on you. God is the same way. Honor Him. He'll remember you when you call on Him. Gift-giving helps to establish and maintain relationships.

But, even better than that, God has set forth His plan to keep you so that you will not need to call on Him because of crises that arise from disobedience or falling out of relationship. God says the Just shall live by faith. He expects us to live from faith to faith, not from crisis to crisis. The critical situations that arise in so many lives are from not honoring God. But instead robbing God, which opens the door for the *spirit of poverty* or some other negative force to come in.

You're calling on God, whose financial hands may be previously tied by you because you didn't honor Him and His laws and principles of giving. You have in essence tied your own hands, too. Now you can't buy that house. You want that new car, or your health may be failing. So you call on God. When your hands were free and you were living in that high place, what did you do? Like that woman on the cliff, did you devise evil and disobedience? Or have you continuously and consistently honored God? We all want to receive honor. We want to be honored--, whether job recognition or praise and positive attention at home or church.

The way to get honor is to give honor first. If you need to, ask for Wisdom on how to give honor. God gave Solomon riches and honor because Solomon asked for Wisdom, (1 Kings 3:13). Look at what comes in the package with Wisdom.

- Riches.
- Honor.
- Length of days.

Do as Solomon did; ask God for Wisdom.

We honor God in our giving, but we cannot give God Wisdom. If you've ever tried to talk God into or out of anything, you know what I mean. His Wisdom far surpasses ours and He won't give into our vain thinking. Even Abraham gave up trying to talk God out of destroying Sodom and Gomorrah. God has crowned us with glory and further honors us by giving us everything good. But we honor God not from our mind by trying to help Him be God, but by paying the tithe and giving of our increase.

Length of Days

In the Wisdom Package, God promised Solomon and us that if we keep His statutes, He would lengthen our days, (1Kings 3:14). Man has ever wanted youth and long life. Ponce de Leon discovered Florida while searching for the Fountain of Youth. God is the saint's fountain of youth. Living waters flow from His throne, (Revelations 22:1), and the times of refreshing are with the Lord, (Acts 3:19). As we serve the Lord, we are promised to walk without weariness and to run without becoming faint. God's got it all.

Honoring God by keeping commandments will lengthen and enhance our Earth walk. One way we honor God is in our tithing and offerings.

Both the Old Testament and New Testament say that one who does not honor mother and father will be cursed. God is Father; He is to be honored. God is El Shaddai, the Many Breasted One, so He is our mother, in a sense. Honor thy Father and Mother.

If thou will walk in my ways to keep my statutes and my commandments as thy father David did walk, then I will lengthen thy days. (1 Kings 3:14)

So it is the wise man that honors God. Length of days is in Wisdom's right hand and in Her left hand, riches and honor (Proverbs 3:18). Wisdom holds riches and honor, not the other way around. Riches does not hold Wisdom and honor. The rich are not always wise, nor are they always honorable. With all the money in the world, you cannot buy honor. You can buy knowledge, that is, get an education, but you won't know what to do with it without Wisdom, James 1:5 tells us that God will give Wisdom not only for free, but also freely and generously, if we ask.

Neither is honor holding Wisdom and riches. Holding on to money instead of tithing and offerings is neither wise nor honorable, (Malachi 3:10). We would look like morons trying to hold a gun on God to rob Him. You would look like an idiot cartoon character trying to trick God out of a blessing. It cannot be done. Not paying the tithe is one such foolish act. It seems to have no repercussion but, it does have very grave consequences. Whether the trustees or the pastor of your church calls you in to speak to you about disobedience in tithing or not, you should be able to manage yourself, *yourself*. Sadly, many Christians would become offended if someone spoke to them about the thing that is diminishing the quality of their life, and the very thing that would keep them out of God's presence.

Honor is not holding Wisdom and riches, (Proverbs 3:16). Therefore, honor causes one to let go of what does not belong to him. If you were holding a stolen object that the police were looking for, you'd give it to them, wouldn't you? When God is requiring

His tithes and expecting offerings, if you're still holding on to them, they are stolen. Do you respect and honor the police? Yes. But more than God?

The spiritually sane man says, *"No."*

Honor gives to God what is His. Pay the tithe without someone standing over your shoulder. This is the same honor that causes you to write the check for your credit card bill or mortgage payments without repeated letters and calls from the lender. Just as you want good credit in the natural, you want good credit with God.

Honor causes you, even when you are by yourself, to put the money in the self-pay slot in the parking lot, or in the meter on the street. Honor is the behavior you exhibit when no one is looking. Honor is how you treat your wife or husband when they are not in the room. Honor is a decision. It works by love and respect. It takes discipline.

Honor God and He will honor you. He will honor the request of the disciplined. He will not refuse you.

Exercise

For thought:

1. Are my conditions favorable for God to jump in with me when I call, or have I tied His hands?
2. Am I really an honorable person?
3. Do I behave honorably even when no one is looking?

Very highly recommended **AMONG SOME THIEVES** by this author. https://a.co/d/cw6Pxnp

You Haven't Planted Anything

You haven't planted anything for God to help you harvest, but you're still asking Him for blessings. This should be simple. He has to refuse you. It's similar to going to a bank to draw from your account, but you haven't put anything in it. You've made no deposits. It's the same as being Saved but having no *works*. Being Saved opens the account, but you've never paid a tithe or even given an offering. Those are the deposits into your account. Thank God you're Saved. At least you have an account. Not being Saved at all would be comparable to not having an account. Why waste time asking? You wouldn't drive up to the teller window at the bank to withdraw money where you don't bank. The only way you could get money out of that bank is to rob it. And that's exactly why keeping the tithe is robbery.

Or it's like having a job, but you haven't been to work, therefore you draw no paycheck on payday. How can you expect God to do anything for you if you haven't done anything for yourself? Note, I said you haven't done anything for *yourself*.

When you manage your life and take care of yourself, that is your proving ground. Then you can use what you learn to help others who have not gotten where you are. Haven't you noticed that your testimony helps people who are going through what you went through? That's why you went through it because God deemed you strong enough to endure. Haven't you noticed that people you attract and people you seem to be most helpful to are those who are going through things you know something about? You learned how to handle yourself in a situation, then you can share the testimony and what you experienced with others. What you have learned in going through is not how you handle the problem, but it is how God took care of you in the situation. It is how you, through Christ, overcame. Now you share, testify, witness to, and teach others who may not have yet learned how to be Christ-sufficient. Not self-sufficient, as the world teaches, but Christ-sufficient.

Christr-Sufficiency

I can do all things through Christ which strengthens
me. (Philippians 4:13)

I can do all things through Christ, that is
through the Christ-sufficiency. Christ is not Jesus's last
name; it is His anointing. Even if you are not saved,
you have anointing. Especially if you are saved, and
really especially if you are Spirit-filled and among the
called and *chosen,* you have anointing. There is more
than one kind of anointing, but the Christ Anointing is
what allows you to do *all things.* Anointing without
works is vain and of no effect and works without
anointing is both tiring and futile. We should all
endeavor to be Christ-sufficient, which means
anointing-sufficient. That means recognizing the
power of God that He graces us to use to cause
Kingdom work to happen here in the Earth.

God said to Paul, *My Grace is sufficient*
because of Christ (2 Corinthians 12:9). Because of the
anointing, because of the Grace, we can do all things,
all things through the anointing, all things through
Christ, all things by the sufficiency given by God. One

definition of Grace is the ability to use something that's not yours for free, for a time, as in the grace period, when you forget to pay your insurance premium, the policy stays in effect for a while until you can get that payment to the company.

After seeking the Kingdom and doing Kingdom work, we are allowed to live in the overflow. If we stop thinking about ourselves and seeking God for our personal selves so much and do the work that He has called us to do:

- We will have Christ-sufficiency. And that is *all* sufficiency.
- We will have abundance.
- We will not be refused when asking for tools, instruments, items, even people and money for Kingdom work.

But what have you done for yourself? What have you planted in the field from which you want to harvest? Do you just plan to beg, and glean from the leftovers all your life? Is that your plan? Surely it can't be.

It is true that God knows your heart. Saying, *Lord, if you bless me, I will bless everyone I meet*, is not going to sway Him. He knows you only want $1,000,000 so you can quit work, travel, and shop, no matter what your mouth is saying as to why you want it.

Planning financially and in other ways is the step that clues God that you are progressing from the *me*-mentality. In the me- mentality, you plant seed in yourself, only. You plant and sow seed in your own field. You try to harvest, but it is only you and your field. Not being able to get everything you need from one field, disappointments may come.

In the Wilderness, the Israelites got tired of the manna every day, which they had because they weren't sowing in any outside fields, it was just them. (I hope that sparks your missions outlook.) Except for God's Grace, Mercy, and sovereignty, they never would have gotten meat. In your own flesh you have very little if any increase; we can't diversify or multiply like God. In Genesis He said that we should be fruitful and multiply, but are we? You can add; look at your savings account 1 + 1. You can definitely subtract. Man can divide, but are you obeying God and multiplying?

God is. God can.

Sowing only in yourself is a form of idolatry, depending on yourself, believing that you yourself can do all things in and of yourself. It's saying you don't need anybody; do you know you need God? Only through Christ you can do all things. You have Christ-sufficiency, but if you haven't sown into the Kingdom of God, then it would be inappropriate to show up with harvesting equipment to reap from a field where nothing has been planted. Or if something had been planted in your field which could sustain or prosper that kind of seed, even if it were your field, just your field cannot sustain the kind of harvest that you want me to live to do what God has called you to do.

Now plant.

Once the tithe is paid, then the seed can be planted. A dormant field with static soil can repel seed. Have you ever tried to water a plant that you've forgotten for weeks or months? All the water runs right through it because the soil has hardened. You have to work that Earth, moisturize it, and put nutrients in it before planting if you even have seed. But most who haven't planted, besides having inappropriate soil have *eaten* their seed.

Soil that is hardened because of nonuse, season after season cannot *receive* seed. Seed being the Word. Yes, I'm saying the soil of your heart may be hardened if you are not working the principles of God. The Tithers are getting revelation of the Word of God and taking off with it. They're the ones with the awesome testimonies. Then there are the non-tithers, often, they are the non-testifiers. They hear the Word, and if attentive, they add something else to their collection of knowledge, their *information*. They may even write it down. But true revelation is for the Tithers. The Tithers have beforehand proved to God that they have faith to mix with the Word. That faith was both proven and activated by the act of tithing. When they mix their faith with the Word, they bring forth success, victory and testimonies.

Adam and Eve tithed. That's why the Garden of Eden reseeded itself. How can I say that? Why would God suddenly tell Cain and Abel about first fruits and proper giving, but skip Adam and Eve?

Even the Earth *tithes* and gives offerings of itself to reseed itself. The Garden yielded fruit, and automatically in the fall and the harvest time, seeds drop, spores take flight, and leaves fall to mulch the ground.

In order to plant spiritually, you must tithe. The field is plowed or prepared, tilled by the tithe (as it were). If the field is ready, then it can be planted, in season. The Offering plants the seeds. The tithe is for blessings past. The offering is for blessings expected and desired in the future. Sowing in the offering is the same as planting. Sow in the offering, so when you ask God, He will not refuse you on the grounds of not having planted.

God rebukes the weeds in the growing season. That's another benefit of the tithe. Spiritual *weeds* may be because of blatant sin and works of the flesh. Chronic and habitual sin can destroy even a heavily planted field. If you're faithful with the tithes, as God has said, He will rebuke the Devourer. Then Scripture says if we *faint not* then we shall harvest, and God is

Lord of the Harvest. *Faint not* equals *sin not* --.as much as it's in you, and don't give up. No one is perfect and sin free, but we all, through Christ attempt to live holy.

Now if you are to harvest, you need God; He is Lord of the Harvest.

Make a joyful noise unto God all ye lands,

(Psalm 66:1).

You are the land; you are the earthen vessel. You've been placed here to do good works on behalf of God. You have given Him authority to use you in service, and He has given you authority, to do works. You are the land. You can grow, be cultivated and render a harvest. You can be planted with seed and give birth to ideas, revelation, deliverance, prayer, and ministry, as you have been gifted by God. You are the land. The land was to be plowed, tilled, and tended. The land must be worked. If it lays dormant, it will harden or be taken over by weeds and thistles.

God gives the seed. He gives seed to the Sower and bread to the eater, (Isaiah 53:10). The weeds still try to grow. God rebukes the Devourer, that is the weeds in the field, the predators, the animals that eat that kind of seed, and immature seedlings. He is your protector.

Your offerings of praise, service, and finances afford you the luxury of having the Devourer rebuked. It offers you protection. I say luxury because God does it for you. You don't have to do it all by yourself. Your offerings, of both finance and self toward the saved and unsaved, causes God to give you protection and favor, but you still must do some of the work yourself. You must tithe and give offerings so you can reap in season.

It would be unusual, if you are tithing and ministering to others for God not to supply your needs.

You may see so many who give and give and don't seem to have. You may be thinking that you don't want to be like that. Then don't. Those people are probably not asking God for anything. Everyone is not materialistic, but as God has promised us, all things that pertain to life and godliness, the man of God should never have to do without, unless God is correcting his character by withholding certain things for a season. Judge not. But if you ask not, you will not receive, and if you ask out of order, you will not receive, (James 4:2-3). That may mean how you ask, as well as the order of your life and lifestyle when you ask.

If you are not being served, it may be because you are not serving.

God is faithful. He will not refuse His own. He will not refuse His faithful. He will not refuse His *called.* He will not refuse His *chosen.* You do not have to be called to preach in order to have a relationship with God. No. The veil is rent (Mark 15:38). God wants a personal relationship with each of us. Moreover, <u>you</u> decide what level of relationship you want to have with the Father. You decide by your actions, your faith, your faithfulness, your obedience, your willingness, whether or not you plant, how and what you plant, the way you treat money and other potential idols, the way you treat people, those of the faith and the unsaved.

You have power. You have power because you have authority in the Earth. You have a lot to say in whether God is going to refuse you or bless you.

Highly recommended *When The Devourer Is Rebuked,*

https://a.co/d/gcl4VIF and

Let Me Have A Dollars' Worth https://a.co/d/h4PR4Nq

both by this author.

A Form of Godliness

Having a form of godliness, but denying the power thereof, (2 Timothy 3:5).

Appearing affluent but not having money or using money to its fullest is a *form* of godliness. Appearing affluent but not using money to its full potential on your behalf, is foolish. If the mall has a dress for $100, but the catalog has the very same dress for $70., which one is the better purchase to make? (Assuming that this is not a special occasion wear-once outfit), where will you get the most for your dollar? How will you use the money to its maximum potential? In which situation will you use your money wisely, provided you need a new dress and have budgeted for such? That's easy, isn't it?

What if the nice dress cost $100 and a cheap copy that would fall apart after the first wash costs $50? Which dress would you buy? That's also easy, isn't it?

What if you made $1000 last week and the tithe (at 10%) was $100, but instead you put $50.00 in the offering plate? The $50 check is a cheap *imitation of a tithe;* it is a *form* of godliness. You filled out and put in a tithe envelope. You wrote a check and put in or put in some cash. It looked like you tithed, but *after the first washing--*, applying the water of the Word to your action, God knows you didn't tithe. Like the cheap dress, will your relationship with God fall apart? Did you pay the $50 as your tithe so you could buy that $100 dress? Should you pay the tithe in full or buy the dress? If either that was a difficult decision *or* you made the wrong decision, which was to buy the dress instead of paying the tithe, then you just failed a spiritual test.

The Church *Appearance*

There you are in beautiful church attire; your sanctified stuff—coordinated pumps and handbag, wearing a hat so decorated, you could set it on the hotel brunch table with the rest of the fresh fruit displayed. You have driven up in a brand-new luxury car. But then what? You've short-changed God on the tithe last week and now it's an offering week--, you bring $10. God is not impressed. That doesn't even make up for the stolen tithe money from last week. Even though you consider this $10. an offering, **it's not an *offering* until after you've paid your tithe.** And you're still $40 short from the last time you got paid. What if the pastor called you into the office for a reprimand if you fell behind in your tithing? Many churches do. The pastor is, after all, concerned for your soul.

You could go to hell for robbery, that's where the two on the crosses on either side of Jesus were headed. There was more than one cross. There were more than just two others up there with Jesus. And there were more than just robbers up on those crosses. Further, there were certainly more than three crosses; there were crosses as far as the eye could see, on any given day. The Romans did everything on a very large scale.

But you're saved, so you can't go to hell. Okay, if you're saved, why aren't you tithing?

What is all this religious dressing up for church about anyway? When Old Testament folks worshipped, they took **livestock** with them, to slaughter! How many Chanel or Armani suits do you think came to church then?

People have so much pomp, but find themselves under the circumstances, too often. God is glad you came to church, but He is not impressed with appearances and *forms of godliness*. Was it better for God to see you dressed up, than for Him to receive His tithes and offering? More truthfully, was it more important for the other people at church to see you looking good, than for God to see you tithing?

Remember, not tithing properly was Cain's downfall and it was the cause of Ananias's and Sapphira's demise, too.

Dressing up your flesh and bringing it to church, does not impress God. Bring spiritual things to church. Designer suits and handbags are not spiritual. Bring your soul, which includes your mind. Bring your gifts, and those things that you intend to consecrate to the Lord. Bring with you that which you will use to worship the Lord in Spirit and in Truth.

If you want to impress me, buy *me* a Jaguar (or a Tesla). If you want to impress God, bring **Him** the new auto and/or the Armani suit, (or the equivalent). God rejoices in the prosperity of His servants.

Not paying the tithe is not a sign of prosperity.

What if church was carried out privately in booths, where no one saw the other person's outfit, but the amount of our offering check was posted beside your name on a public bulletin board? What would you wear, and how much would you give then?

How about a drive through church where you didn't even have to get out of your car, but as you drove through the amount of the tithe you paid would be read aloud and blare through the speakers for all to hear? What would you wear then? What would you tithe?

When you're alone at home or in your car, what do you wear to listen to your favorite radio, TV or internet evangelist? I'm not saying that the well-dressed don't tithe. Neither am I saying that the tithers aren't well-dressed. Lack of generosity do not always correlate to high fashion. Some, for example, who tune in to Christian radio or television broadcasts, behave as though they are doing the minister *a favor* by listening or watching. They never send in a penny to support the radio or television program, and chances are good that they aren't sitting in their homes in designer clothes while listening to the Word of God. In that case, the person wasn't dressing up for God, if they were, they'd put on their church clothes, fruit-topped hat included before turning on the radio, internet, or TV. They are dressing for other people when they come out in public.

Too many non-tithers are spending God's money on clothes, shoes, cars, things and stuff to impress people. And there are too many non-tithers.

Christian programming is not like the world's. Although many times, we have to go through the world's system to reach the masses. There are no advertisements or commercials; the preacher/teacher and his ministry pay for the entire program. The TV network is not paying the minister to be on the air. The ministry is paying the TV station because they want to get the Word out. Airtime, radio/TV/internet time can be very expensive. Conversely, secular television stars and radio hosts make hundreds of thousands of dollars per episode because folks like you support the companies and manufacturers that advertise on those secular programs.

You support the mall, the grocery stores and the car companies, then *they* support **secular** television and radio. These same manufacturers and businesses that you support, support **secular** programming, but give an excuse to not sponsor Christian programming, under the guise of not wanting to offend anyone. Shouldn't we Christians be offended by anyone who denies and wants to deny our God?

The mall, car dealer and shoe store are not *gods*.

If you think about it, you are really working against yourself. The products that you buy support the kind of TV that you **don't** want your child to watch, the kind of programs that put the ideas in teenagers' heads, and then we turn to God for God to fix the problems the world creates. If would be better to support the efforts of the people who work for God.

This is your case? No wonder life doesn't seem to be working. No wonder God seems to be refusing you. It's the same as devising evil when on a high place and tying God's hands while you're up there.

Honor... *Again*?

Christian teachers, preachers, evangelists, and music ministers rely on your honor to bless them, after they've blessed you. They are relying on you and your honor. Most didn't choose ministry, **God chose them** (John 15). But God didn't choose them to suffer financially. Preachers are *not* in ministry for punishment.

There are no Emmy's for Christian teaching and preaching programs. There is no rating system for best show. That's because there are no commercials and no advertisers, (under normal conditions). You'd be pretty irritated when as the Spirit is moving, your favorite Christian program cut to a car commercial, with barely dressed models, dragging you back into your flesh. Do you think you could get back in the Sprit before the program concluded? Maybe you don't really watch commercials, so the (hypothetical) car ad airs, and you leave the room to get a glass of water. The telephone rings, and you forget to come back. You never get the full message, or impact of the Christian program. Either way, the effect of the ministry is diminished. To avoid such disasters, Christian television is supposed to be supported by the people who watch it and get fed by it, Christians.

There you are on your honor, soaking up all the Word from every ministry you can get your eyes and ears on; but keeping your money in your wallet for the mall. What has the mall done for you spiritually, and what can the mall do for you, eternally?

Answer that. _____

You should be sending in offerings to all the ministries you watch and listen to. By that I do not merely mean ordering a CD, a download, or a book. Yes, order teaching materials, but a real offering means sending in a love gift to support that ministry's good works, expecting no gift back from them. Not an ink pen, a bookmark, a tape, or handkerchief. Nothing. We should not have to be promised something to send something. That's not really an offering, that's a *purchase* unless you send in over and above the amount that is asked for.

Are you dubbing Christian music. What is the musician or singing man or woman of God supposed to *eat*? You have a spiritual responsibility to bless people who bless you. What if your boss figured out a way to **not** bless you on payday? What if this week he Xerox the same check that he gave you last week? That's what you're doing when you dub Christian music. You're asking the recording artist to Xerox the original check that purchased the recording in the first place. This is what you're asking them to do, so they can feed their family and *live*. Those artists expect that they will get paid when their music is heard, and every time their music goes into a new home. If it were your recording, wouldn't you?

How many Christian books and workbooks have you photocopied so you don't have to invest $10 or $15 in your spiritual growth? You want the spiritual growth for yourself, but your behavior is as though you don't want the author, who is really your *teacher* in that season, to get paid. Is that selfish or what? And whose copier did you use to copy those 140 pages? Oh, you did it at work, didn't you? That's stealing times stealing. In the world, you'd gladly pay $25., and up for a bestselling novel or book that tells of murder, mayhem, mischief and other such *much of nothings*. You'd pay as much, or more for a cookbook; Christian booksellers should not have to mark their prices down so Christians will buy them. What is the *spirit of cheapness* lending itself to dishonor that comes over people when they profess being **saved**? When you were in the world you would spend money on whatever you wanted, but now that you're saved and called to be a wise steward, things that pertain to life you'll pay for, but things that pertain to godliness, you act as though they should be free. What of that mentality has changed since you got saved? Nothing. That's the way you've always treated God, the man of God, the people of God, and the things of God. That's why it took you so long to get saved in the first place. Nothing has changed. But you really need to change and seek some prosperity in the mind of your soul so that God can stop refusing you.

If you have no money and no means, that TV or radio broadcast is a way for you to glean from the Word of God, but you are expected to grow up spiritually, financially and responsibly. Then you are to become a blessing to the Kingdom, just as mature, generous, giving saints whom you probably don't even know have invested into _your_ spiritual salvation and growth. If you have means but are not faithful to send offerings, where you are being fed, that's the same as being a thief and a robber. If you are watching Christian television but not supporting Christian television, then we only _appear_ to be a Christian.

Do you pay when you are finished eating in a restaurant, or do you just walk out?

If we have sown spiritual things among you, is it too much if we reap material things from you?

(1Corinthians 9:11)

People who steal cable are in the world but stealing the Word of God is another issue, and it does not profit.

The Word is free, you might say. Is it? Why did Jesus have to pay so much if it's free?

The _real_ man or Woman of God is not up for popularity contest. Neither is he tarrying in the Word to receive revelation _for money_; it's his _calling_. Based

49

on how the average professed Christian gives, there are a lot more and surer ways to make money. It is his job, and he is doing it as unto God. Anyone who has a job that they feel *called* to do, will understand that. If you were or are in your purpose, you have no problem grasping this concept.

Those who think the man of God is working for money are people who work for money.

Book 4 in this series is: ***Do Not Work for Money***
https://a.co/d/iwMIKYk

Can't Trust That

A common excuse for not giving is that you can't trust preachers. Then don't watch the ones you can't trust and don't listen to their programs. This way you will not be responsible for blessing their ministry either prayerfully ad/or financially. The man and Woman of God should be well honored and well-fed, over and above clothing designers and car manufacturers.

The Stale Prince

Beyond air, teachers, preachers and evangelists are working full force against many obstacles, not just finances. One formidable obstacle is the *prince of the powers of the air*—the devil. You know from your own life that the enemy will attack whatever will stop you from doing the thing that you're supposed to be doing, especially if it's to the glory of God. If you are receiving teaching or edification from any source, then it is your responsibility to give to those ministries (all that you receive from), to keep them on the air and defeat the prince of the powers of the air. Furthermore, concerning ministries that you watch and listen to in person and over the airwaves, you are not only *accountable* for what they said, but you are also responsible for blessing them for saying it to you, (1 Corinthians 9:11), whether you like it or not.

Church is not a plaything, and neither is the Word of God.

If you've ever listened to an AM radio station, it seems that when the Minister gets to the good part, the signal diminishes. If people were supporting the good ministries with offerings and donations, programs could be broadcast on stations with stronger signals. You could enjoy it more and it would bless more people. If all the people who really listen and are ministered to by Christian programs gave as they should, Christian broadcasting would far surpass secular programming. We'd have the best equipment, the best stations, and would be able to buy the best signals and those who listen would be blessed abundantly by God. Also, those who give would be blessed abundantly by God. This is how it should be. No man of God should have to broadcast on less than the best because of finances.

The ever so stale prince of the powers of the air has been doing the same old things ever since he fell like lightning. When will we recognize his tactics and defeat him?

Keep it Real

Stop trying to *look* like a Christian and **be** a Christian. Your fashion statement is only a modern-day *form of godliness*.

As teenagers, my friends and I would plan weeks in advance what we were to an event such as a concert. It's hard to believe that we actually planned what we'd wear to sit in the dark and watch performers sing. What difference does it make what *we* wore to sit in the theater? It wasn't until I was a young adult at an R&B concert and sat behind a man and Stetson cowboy hat that I realized that there is a certain attire for certain events, and that wasn't it. I also realized that unless I'm getting an honorarium and 10% of the gate, it doesn't matter what *I* wear to a concert.

In the same way, God is the focus and the purpose of church. As long as I'm clean, comfortable, and decent, what does it matter what I wear to church? What matters is that I come with the right heart, in the right spirit, and with the right motive to worship the Lord. All else is deceit or fluff. Clothes and appearances will not come before God in my life. Appearing godly or *looking* holy will not be my focus. I will be who God called me to be. I will give honor where honor is due, and I will bless the men and women of God who are worthy because they feed me spiritually.

I Have a Servant

But more to the point, let's not deny the power in financial godliness. Why isn't money serving you? Money is rebellious. *What?* How can that be? Money has taken on a life of its own when it's got you doing things for **it**. You get up at ungodly hours to go to work, but you may not even want to. Or you hate your job, but you work for the money. You do ungodly things to earn, win, or even steal money. You go where the drive for money tells you to go. You do what money tells you to do. Money can be rebellious, and it can be causing you to be rebellious too.

You are to bring that rebellious money to the House of God and consecrate it for service. That money is supposed to serve God, the Kingdom of God, the House of God, **and you**. As an affirmation, I say, *Money comes up to me and serves me*. The Bible says in Luke 16, don't serve unrighteous Mammon.

Don't serve money because it's supposed to serve you.

Money serves God, and we are created in His image and likeness, so it should serve us too. How does money serve God? Good question--, He owns all of it, and everything that He owns serves Him. Everything He owns obeys Him. Jesus walked on the water and now He walks on streets of gold. It's all His. He can do with it as He pleases.

At the name of Jesus every knee will bow. Bowing implies serving. All things serve the Lord, and us too. Fish of the sea, fowls of the air, beasts of the field. The Red Sea served Moses; the Jordan served Joshua, the Rock in Hebron served the Israelites, the gourd served Jonah. Both living and things inanimate serve us. Money should serve us. You have a servant, at least one. It's money.

Form and Fashion

Aren't you tired of just *looking* good? Beth looks good all the time, but she complains about a lack of money and being behind on bills. She doesn't look needy. I'm not suggesting that we walk by sight. But if we did, we'd have to give money to every pan handler on every street corner. Beth was investing her energy, money and time into *looking* good and *appearing* godly, but she had no <u>finances</u> to back it up.

Appearing needy is not the answer either. Don't go to the opposite extreme. Cindy dressed her children in tight old clothes when she brings them to visit certain well-off relatives. Her plan is that the relatives, in sympathy for the kids will give her money. Well-off relatives have discernment, and they have Wisdom. That's why they're well-off.

Over time, the woman became a joke in that family.

Who Do You Think You Are?

Jesus did not appear affluent while here on Earth. He gave no concern to the latest in togas, sandals or chariots. He said, *"I came that you may have life and have it more abundantly."* He didn't say He came, that you might *appear* to have life more abundantly. Yet, if you have *managed* the church appearance, if you have managed to look church-worthy, if you have managed to fool some of the people--, who have you really fooled? Not God, and hopefully not yourself.

I will not buy a new outfit every time I go to a function. If who I already am isn't already part of my wardrobe, then who am I? And who am I willing to *become*?

In Bible times, who you are was reflected in how you dressed. Kings wore purple because it was very expensive, and they could afford it. Back then, your clothes were your identity. Look in Leviticus to see how God specified the priest to be attired. God is very precise. God is a perfectionist. That's why He's perfecting you and me. But who are you? Have you become who you're supposed to be? Do you think the church clothes make you a church person? Do you really want to *be* a church person, or would you rather be a Christ-like person and a disciple?

What do you wear? Are you one kind of someone Monday through Friday and then become Super Saint on Sunday? Who are you fooling? Not God. Are you looking affluent and Godly on Sundays, but in actuality have no power at all? You aren't just *appearing* Godly when while life defeats you? That's a *form* of godliness, denying the power thereof.

A woman came to my office so that I could fix her teeth because God had called her to preach. I don't know if He did or not, that's between that person and God. But she wanted a complete makeover, and she wasn't even going to look the same anymore. Did God called her to minister to people in her current station in life? Or did He call her to make herself into someone completely different and then attempt to minister to the people in *that* station of life? Or did God call her to make herself over so she could *attempt* to minister to people that she would now look like, but have no common ground with? I was confused. Maybe God just called her to fix her teeth. I don't know, but

I'm saying just be who you are. There are people with Billy Bob teeth who need ministry. If a person with the toothpaste model smile shows up in a Billy Bob Assembly, that might intimidate the Billy Bobs, making the ministry of none effect.

Be yourself.

Godliness leads to abundance. Not a *form* of abundance, not the *appearance* of abundance, but real abundance. Abundance is enough to share. It is scriptural to reap so abundantly that you can be a blessing and be blessed.

There is power in abundance. There is power in money. It is your defense. It is one thing that can move God to rebuke the Devourer for you. **I do not see in the Bible any other way to have the Devourer rebuked other than to pay God His 10%**. Some argue that tithing is not Scriptural --, well if it is the only way to have the Devourer rebuked, then I'm going to tithe. If not, please tell me where the Devourer is; what has changed? Has he already been sent to the Abyss?

Do not deny the power in your giving and in your sowing. You shall have power to get wealth and power to **keep** wealth. The Bible says that a man shall reap in joy and enjoy the fruits of his labor; it is a gift from God, (Ecclesiastes 3:13). If you look Godly, sound Godly, but you're not using money to its full potential on your behalf and enjoying it, then you're not being wise and you're not being Godly.

Don't be a fake.

That's a bold statement. Yes it is. If God only *looked* Godly, dressed in white raiment and had on a robe so tough that the train of it filled the Temple, and as He ascended and descended on clouds, had angels all around Him--, when He made the storms and the seas obey Him, and the sun and the moon stand still, but was **broke**, would He still be God?

If He set the table before you and then asked you to get the check and He'd pay you back later, **would he still be God**? What if He took you shopping for all the things that pertain to life and for godliness, and put it on *layaway*? If God had a trillion-dollar deficit in His heavenly budget, streets of gold, gates of Pearl and unpaid invoices piled up around the throne, would He still be godly?

If He gave those good gifts spoken of in the New Testament but charged them on a credit card, if He took you to the Heavenly grocery store to supply all your needs and they wouldn't take His check or His credit card was over the limit, would He still be God if He didn't make money also serve Him? Would He still be God? If He did everything, He was supposed to do about everything and everyone on Earth, but let money run all over Him, is the He still the *man*, is He still God? Is He still godly?

The sane man will say, *"No."*

Yet too many who profess Christianity have no abundance or prosperity to back up **who** and *whose* they say they are.

What if God frequented lottery lines and casinos to get more money for His Kingdom? Would He still be Godly? God wants to know that about you too.

Anything that has power over you has the potential to be a *god* over you. You must exert power and authority over money, else it might exert its influence over you. You must exert full authority over money, just as God does. Are you taking Dominion and Authority over everything in your life, ***except money?*** What's so mystical and scary about money? Nothing. Take authority.

Power

Money is a defense. It is a weapon of your warfare. Yet sometimes in warfare you need some rebuking done on your behalf. You want the Devourer rebuked, don't you? Then pay your tithes. Just as when you were a child, you wanted your parent to correct, stop and or punish your brother for picking on you and pulling your hair. Your brother was wrong, so you wanted your brother "rebuked." You knew right from wrong. You knew what was needed, and maybe you didn't have the power, the authority, or the ability to do the *rebuking* yourself. Maybe your big brother or sister was physically overpowering you, just as the devil sometimes seems to be spiritually more than you can handle. You may not think you have rebuking power over the devil, but since God does, then in Jesus's Name, you do too.

If you want abundant harvests for your family and your friends, and your needs, and to be a blessing to the Kingdom, then give cheerfully, abundantly, and it shall be returned to you 30, 60, 100-fold depending on your faith, (Mark 4:8). In your giving is your power.

In Deuteronomy 8:18 God gives us the *power to get wealth.* Then we know it takes power, energy, force, purpose to get wealth. If in Malachi 3:10 God says He will rebuke the Devourer, then we know it takes power, energy, force, and purpose to **keep** wealth. The Bible even talks about *power to enjoy your wealth.*

Every man also, to whom God hath given riches and wealth. And have given him power to eat thereof, and to take the portion, and to rejoice in his labor. This is the gift of God. (Ecclesiastes 5:19)

How much power is *rebuking* power? I think here it is more like rebuking authority. When God speaks, and at the Name of Jesus knees bow under His power and also under our authority. We have authority to use His power, which is the use of His **Name**.

When I use certain names, I have advantages, authority, power, and potential that I might not otherwise have. For instance, when I used the name American Express, I can charge thousands of dollars' worth of products and services when I don't at that time have thousands of dollars in my wallet. When I use my husband's last name and present my medical insurance card, I receive health care at no cost to me. I may not have a health policy in my name, but I have health insurance in my name, but I have the full benefits because I'm using his name.

I can do these things because I have *relationship* and that relationship gives me authority as if I were that person. You do it all the time. You use names and relationships to identify yourself or to receive favor and honor. When you use the company credit card, you get the same respect and treatment as though you were the CEO of the company (almost). You say things like, *"I work for so and so."* Or, *"My friend or I belong to,.."* Or *"Yes, I'm born again. I'm a son or a daughter of God."* It's called authority, it's the same as if God said it.

Every knee shall bow, and things shall serve me.

Different names have different authority levels. At the Name of Jesus mountains and trees move, storms stop, things happen. The Name of Jesus is available to all who are saved or born again. If you are one of His and you are in relationship, then you can use the Name of Jesus. The names of God have different attributes. Sometimes He is my Healer, sometimes He is my Provider, sometimes He's my Banner or my Protector. He is Jehovah Lord. He does not refuse me the use of His Name, which has the power and the attribute that I need. Because of that, I move in real godliness and real power, not just a form of, or the *appearance* of power, or godliness.

Exercise:

What has Christian programming done for you spiritually?

How has Christian media programming impacted your view, expectations, and relationships with Eternity?

Have you honored all ministers who have labored in the Word for you? Yes, or no?

Have you honored ministers you've enjoyed on TV, radio or Internet? Yes, or no?

Important: If you've used media, TV, radio, or Internet ministry to only get out of the bind of not knowing what you were going to teach in Sunday school or teach at Bible study, that's the same as copying off another's paper in school, unless you pay for the education that you received.

You do not want a doctor, or a lawyer that cheated in school, do you? So what makes you think your Sunday school pupils and pew members want a teacher who copied off someone else's paper? If a radio, internet, TV minister has served you as your teacher, then you must honor them. Pay them? They have labored in the Word and are actually worthy of double honor, (1 Timothy 5:17)

Exercise:

Are you honoring those who speak into your life?

Air Offering

While at the sports shoe store in the mall, I saw many products marked, *air*. There was Air Jordan, Air Nike, to name a couple. I've heard of grabbing some air, as in skiing, surfing or snowboarding. *Air* must be a good thing, but there's so much attention given to air as though it were just discovered. In the process of living, respiration is breathing air, it's breathing out and in, and it is a good thing. But *waiting* to inhale or exhale is not. Air in babies' digestive tract is not a good thing, nor in adults who've eaten too many beans.

For saints who aspired to meet God, to be in the presence of God and please God in their offering, **air** is definitely not a good thing.

There are many ways, and there are many levels in which we can experience God and the presence of God. How do we know we are close to God or even in His presence? And how do we get *there*, or even closer?

Since ancient times, folks have always wanted God's presence to guide them, protect them and keep them. So God instructed the Israelites to build Him a tent of meetings.

And let them make me a sanctuary that I may dwell among them, (Exodus 25:8)

In that dwelling there would be three parts, the Outer Court the Inner Court, and the Holy of Holies, where God would meet man on the Mercy Seat. Before Jesus, only the God-appointed priests could enter into the place where God would meet them personally. Jesus died at 3:00 PM one afternoon nearly 2000 years ago, and in so doing, the veil was rent that kept the average Joe from going into the Holy of Holies, (Mark 15:38). Before that time, only His sanctified priest, with much trepidation could go into that place where men could actually meet up with the presence of God.

So as it comes to the Tent of Meetings, there are three parts, Outer Court, Inner Court, and the Holy of Holies.

Today we can experience God in those same three *Courts* outside the church, the Outer Court, on the pew, the Inner Court, and at the altar, the Holy of Holies. In our daily life, we can experience God in any or all of those three ways. Escalation to the highest experience is the desired result. Personally, we can experience Him in our flesh, the Outer Court, and in our soul the Inner Court, and in our spirit, the Holy of Holies. God is searching for folk to worship Him in Spirit and in Truth, (John 4:23). So we should all aspire to reach true spiritual worship.

The Courts

Thanksgiving Court

Anyone can attempt this, even unsaved people. They try to reach God through their flesh. They do the opposite of what the well-known warning says, some even try it at home. Some *only* try it at home, thinking they don't need a church, fellowship, or a pastor.

They may drive past the church and remember something good that happened to them and say to themselves or others that they are thankful. They may even *say* they are thankful to God. They may even **be** thankful to God. If these are mere words, lip service--, this I call the *air offering*. It's just talk or hot air, Posting and reposting recycled memes on the Internet., the saying of convenient or commonly heard things, if your heart is far away from God is only lip service. I don't mean that signs and wonders must follow in order for you to be truly thankful, but where is the heart of the truly thankful? Hopefully not just in the flesh, because flesh is not entering into the presence of God.

Now this I say, brethren, that flesh and blood cannot
inherit the Kingdom of God, neither doth corruption
inherit Incorruption, (1 Corinthians, 15:50)

Are your *air offerings* getting to God? Do air offerings, your little *thank you's* even make it to God? There's a prince of the power of the air whose mission is to block communication that travels via air. Daniel had an air problem when he was in Babylon. Daniel was obedient to God, yet the responses to his prayers from the Heavenlies were blocked. Daniel had to fast to break the power of the prince of the air in order to get the answers to his prayers.

Perhaps you need to do the same. Perhaps you need to tithe to break the works of the prince of the powers of the air. The Bible speaks of fasting and praying in synergy, but tithing is what rebukes the Devourer, and fasting is what broke the power of the prince of the powers of the air for Daniel. That prince and the Devourer are either the very same or from the same camp--, hell. So add fasting and tithing to your prayers, especially when you need to hear from God. Of course, the obedient Christian is tithing at every increase and does not need to be reminded.

The Letter

How will you know if your prayers are being heard by God? And are you hearing His responses back to you? Just as in the natural, there are ways to ask people for things and receive answers and responses from those people. It is the same for God. Some ways are more effective than that of others. Make sure you're praying right. How are you presenting your petitions to Him? You don't only pray at home and sing at church, you're coming into the church with prayer request, aren't you?

Consider the letter (or text), the telephone call (voice or facetime), and the visit (in person). Are you using the equivalent of one of these methods? Evaluate how you're approaching God. How are you presenting your petitions to Him? Make sure you're praying correctly.

If you sent a letter to or an e-mail to someone, they may or may not get it. If there is no return receipt, you don't know if they got it or not, unless the letter comes back to you, then you know they *didn't* get it. If they do get it, you don't know when unless you get the signature on the delivery receipt, but you also don't know if they opened it and you don't know when or if they read it.

We are not suggesting you write got a letter. God is not the guy that is alleged to have a PO Box in the North Pole. The letter is the equivalent of driving past the church, or trying the *air offering* at home in which is just saying or thinking, *I am so thankful*. Much like sending the letter, you may wonder did God get it? Was there enough postage on it? Was there enough *power* (faith) in your prayer to reach God? Did you pray correctly, (James 4:3)? You won't know if God heard it or not until you as the Seeker get a sign or wonder. It could take a miracle or coincidence to get a response to a weak or wrong prayer if you get an answer. Has God responded to your faith or is He acting in Mercy? If you do get an answer or a sign, you may think you're in faith. If you don't get an answer or sign, you may doubt God, or if there is even a God at all.

A Seeker may not know very much or anything at all about God. Doubting Him, one may think that God just didn't answer their prayer, when in reality He may not have heard it, it may not have reached Him. Or, if your request, your letter was delivered, it may still be in the Outer Court, still in God's mailbox (inbox).

There's a lot of interference in the air. Just as with radio, television, Internet, shortwave, cell phones and the like, sometimes the signal is not strong enough for reception. Your need is not clear. There may be static, or you may roll into a dead zone while using your cell phone. Most of the time, television and radio reception is clear, but every now and then there may be an air interference. Often, it's when you're in the middle of an important phone call or receiving valuable information. As a saint of God, you can blame it on the prince of the powers of the air, you can make other arrangements to communicate, or you can take authority over this enemy. The devil wants to block communication both ways, you to God and God to you. You can take authority in the Name of Jesus and say to instruments and gadgets, *You will work, you will serve me.* You can take authority over devils by right action and right words.

Wherein in time spent in time passed, he walked according to the course of this world, according to the Prince of the power of the air, the spirit that now worketh in the children of disobedience,

(Ephesians 2:2)

This *air* enemy, the prince of the powers of the air is there to hold up prayers, answers to prayers and blessings, whenever he can. That is why Daniel had to fast. God released the Mighty Angel to stop the blocking of Daniel's answers to his prayers. You don't think you're spiritually immune to this, do you? Men and women of God are trying desperately to get the Word of God out over the airwaves, the radio, Internet, TV. With your prayers and financial support, we can all be victorious.

Stop *air* interference in your own spiritual life. Air interference is what can happen when you enter into Thanksgiving only. This is the equivalence of just writing God a letter, note, e-mail, or text.

The Call

When you call someone, and talk with him, not an answering machine or voicemail and not a bot--, a live conversation. You know the other person is here in your voice. You get to tell them or ask them something, and they respond, hopefully right then, but at least you have the assurance of knowing that they will think about it or get back to you later.

In proximity and connectivity, the telephone call is the equivalent to praise. When you come into the sanctuary and praise God and bring forth your petition, you **know** that He hears you. You may receive an answer or deliverance from a bondage or oppression right then, or it may come later. If He has to think about it, then you should use that time to repent and meet certain spiritual requirements. Whenever He answers, and because He answers, no matter, how He answers, or whatever His answer may be, you are *sure* that God has heard your voice. We must hear His voice, and we need to know that He heard our voice as we petition, praise and worship. The telephone call is great; as the old ad says, *It's the next best thing to being there.* Spiritually it is the Inner Court.

The Visit

Now, let's talk about being there. The third experience is the visit. It is far better than the letter or the telephone call. You are in the same room with the person and preferably in a conversation. It is being able to look the other person in the eye (were it possible with God). Presenting yourself in person goes far in receiving favorable answers to your needs and petitions.

Consider the banker. How many people have been able to acquire first time bank loans by a letter? *Dear Sir, my name is so and so. Please send me $50,000. My signature is at the end of this letter.* How many have gotten a loan by just a phone call without having had a previous relationship with the bank? The **visit** is what is needed to make this transaction happen. The visit begins relationship. The visit signifies relationship. We go home on holidays to see our mother and our father--, the visit. We honor our grandparents and family elders with the visit.

God *visits* and we should too. We are seeking God. We are walking toward Him, and we are looking for His face. We're *visiting* in our worship. The visit is well-pleasing to God. And it is what we do in the **Holy of Holies.**

To which method would you respond the most favorably or most quickly? The letter, the telephone call, or the visit?

The visit.

You are made in God's image and likeness. God is like that too.

Praise Court

Enter into his gates with Thanksgiving and into his courts with praise. Be thankful unto him and bless his name. Psalm 104:4

We are invited to bring our Thanksgiving and our praise into the Courts of the Lord.

Worship Court

Suddenly, a heavy quiet comes over the room. A hushed, weighted, silence. The Angel of God's Presence is here. God Himself may be present. The din of praise has passed; we have ascended into Worship. The whole Earth keeps silent in His Presence in anticipation that He will Speak.

Speak, Lord.

But the LORD *is* in his holy temple: let all the earth keep silence before him. Habakkuk 2:20

The third phase of the God experience is the Worship. It's when we enter into His presence with Thanksgiving **and** Praise. We don't subtract the Thanksgiving and praise, they are necessary. We enter into worship **with** *both* Thanksgiving and Praise, adding to it, worship. Bless His Name. In worship, whatever you need, God will not refuse you. Not only that--, the devil is NOT in this, he cannot be; it only between you and God, you and your Father. Therefore, the devil cannot interfere either. It is as though you and God are face to face. If not that, you are at least in the same room at the same time. And you know it.

Blessing His name is the worship.

Your Body

Flesh

In a service, we may see the waving of hands and hear the shouts of praise to God. But remember, there is a prince of the powers of the air. Is your praise even getting to God? The Outer Court experience is

Thanksgiving. It is experienced by the Seeker. All that is needed is the seekers anointing. Oh, *what's that?* Something in you feels drawn to something and that something is God, but the Seeker just knows that something greater than self. Hopefully the Seeker knows its spiritual, else, he may feel drawn to the great outdoors or to save the planet. That's God who's doing the drawing. It is not the ecosystem or any near-extinct animals. It is God, and He draws by loving kindness.

The Lord hath appeared of old unto me, saying, yes.
Yay, I have loved thee with an everlasting love.
Therefore, with loving kindness have I drawn thee,
(Jeremiah 31:3)

That first drawing may be experienced in our flesh. We may be tingly, warm or even tearful. It's different for different folk. We need more knowledge of who God is, but. we don't know that. So, until then, in our minds and praise life, we are with two thoughts. One, we think that we aren't as bad as the next guy, and two, we think that's enough.

In Thanksgiving, even though the conversation is *to* God, it isn't *about* others. It's about self. Thanksgiving is still flesh. It's all about me, all about you, all about self, until you can stop thinking of yourself constantly and begin to think of others and about others, you will not step into the Inner Court. It's not until you can focus your thoughts on God that you can enter into the Holy of Holies.

Soul

We can experience God in our soul, mind, will, intellect, and emotions. This is the equivalent of the Inner Court. We can plan and will to meet God and have a mind to meet Him. We can know that *God IS* by our intellect and then set out to experience Him. Our emotions will respond in any number of ways. Excitement, happiness, joy, even sadness due to the weight of sin, if we fall under conviction. The response can range from sorrowful or gleeful tears to hysterical laughter in some services.

The Inner Court experience is equivalent to praise. It is the saved person who can enter into praise, having moved past mere Thanksgiving, in which even the unsaved can participate. We're all taught to say, *thank you* from toddler age on up. Praise is the graduation from Thanksgiving. Praise corresponds to the priestly anointing. It is by this anointing you know that God IS, and you are *called* to Him. You are saved and growing in the things of the Spirit. In Thanksgiving you're still thinking about yourself. When you stop thinking about just yourself, you can leave Thanksgiving and enter into praising **God**. Then He can begin to use you to bless others.

The Inner Court experience is praise. Although it is soulish it is a step up from Thanksgiving, but it *includes* Thanksgiving. It may include flesh responses such as chills and goosebumps, rapid heart rate, heat flush, among others. It's verbal and its vocal. That's why there can be so much crying, yelling or noise in a praise service. It is experienced in the soul. We praise God for all He has delivered us from and for all He has done for us.

Your praise encourages God, but a gift of your treasure states the position of your heart. We pay our tithes as to God as a form of praise. Without paying of the tithe, praise is only Thanksgiving, just an *air offering* without tangible and appropriate gifts to God, praise is just noise. You might as well just give a wave as you do at the baseball or basketball game. Without the tithe, it's merely an *air offering* to God.

(I am not likening an air offering to the wave offering of Exodus 29:24.)

In the Spirit

When you were in the presence of God, you are in the Spirit because flesh cannot enter into worship. When you are in true worship, you are in the Spirit.

The Increase

Air Offering

An air offering is merely hot talk. Hot air, hands waving and crying. But the sacrifice of praise requires a tangible gift. Any attempt to approach God without a tangible gift is the same as bringing in air offering. You might look at the air offering as a dry run, a test, a practice session for the real thing.

The Tithe

I haven't always known what a tithe is. First of all, most of my life. I've never heard anyone pronounce it right. They called it, *tide*. I thought it had something to do with the ocean. I didn't understand for years. I certainly was not going to throw money in the ocean, especially when the Scriptures say to cast your bread upon the waters, (Ecclesiastes 11:1). Hearing the word, *tide* worried me.

I hadn't yet seen the word **tithe** written down and didn't know how to spell it, so I couldn't find it in the Bible, or anything in the Bible about a *tide* as it pertained to money, I knew it wasn't laundry detergent. Nobody brought washing powder to church except Evangelist Jacqueline Jones, who ran the I AM Way church store. *I just didn't understand.*

The day I found out, I purposed in my heart to become a tither. Ironically, I didn't have any money at that time. Why would God show me such an important principle about money at a time in my life when I didn't have any money? Why didn't He show me when I had money?

Because, like so many when I had money, I didn't ask God about anything. I didn't ask God *for* anything. Previously, if and when I talked to God, I'd ask Him *for* money. So, when I had money, why bother God? Money is usually what we ask God for anyway, even saints. If people only ask you for money all day, wouldn't you tire of it? There's so much more to God. Yet we can be so linear, always asking God for the same thing. Your children do it to you too. It gets old, doesn't it?

But when the money ran out, He began showing me the principle of tithing, perhaps to teach me **why** I didn't have any money.

First thing I needed was money in order to tithe. The Scriptures say that God would give me money to tithe. I used my faith to receive seed to sow and sure enough, God was and is still faithful. I started out small and grew week by week. He would put money in my hands to test me. I would **_find_** money or people would just hand me money. I saw a $5 bill on the pavement as I was driving on a one-way street. No cars were behind me, so I backed up and picked it up.

I knew that money was meant for me. There wasn't even any traffic, yet it was only a short time after rush hour.

Bread or Seed?

Then came the tests--, plural; not just one. Bread or seed was the first test. Same test, different opportunities. Is the money that is in your hand bread or is it seed? In the above example of the $5 in the street, that was seed. I sowed it. It wasn't enough to pay a bill or feed me, so it must have been *seed*.

Next test: God was taking me to a new level. The new level was in my giving, in knowledge of the Word and discernment in my spiritual life. This is how you go to a new level. God gives tests.

Remember your college tests? You'll often get multiple choices: A, B, C, All, or Neither. Here was God's new test, bread or seed, or neither.

Neither

I would often get the wrong change at the grocery store, more money than I'd even given the clerk. That was a test. At first, I looked pretty hard at that money in my hand. Once I took two or three steps toward the exit, then the Spirit stopped me. Thank God. That money wasn't bread or seed, it was neither. That was the test. I would give it back, even if it were only a penny. The more I gave back, the more instances came up when God would bless me financially for real. Soon the found money and the too much change amounts begin to increase. The test stepped up. It's easy to give back a dime, but how about $10 or $20 too much change? Especially when you have no money. I continued to give it back. Cashiers and clerks would look at me as though I was from another planet.

God would give me seed to sow and bread to eat and increase my seed sown. I wouldn't have to lie or steal to get it. How is God going to prosper me if the seed of my sowing was stolen money? Accursed offerings do not work on the altar or in the offering basket. If you stole the money to pay for your mother's operation, you just cursed your mother's health and yourself. Stealing for what you think is a good cause, does not justify it. That's theft.

Do you think Joseph's brothers tithed on the 20 pieces of silver they got for his sale to the Midianites? Did Judas on the 30 pieces of silver that he got for Jesus? No, thieves don't tithe. That's how we know them as thieves.

The Counterfeiter

The devil is a counterfeiter. If God gives seed to sow, won't the Devil also try that? Sowing stolen money reaps corruption, destruction and death.

Also, every dollar may not be *from God*. The devil could have been putting money in my hands to stop me from tithing, by roping me back into robbing God and defiling myself. *Whew!* We must stay vigilant.

For he that soweth to his flesh shall of the flesh reap corruption, but he that soweth to the spirit shall of the spirit reap life everlasting. (Galatians 6:8)

I have found money at my feet, hence my affirmation. Money is at my feet; it comes to serve me. Once, when I only had a few dollars of my own, I was in a grocery store line. On the floor in front of me was a $10. bill that the person in front of me had just dropped, unawares. I tapped the shoulder of the person ahead of me and asked, *Did you drop this?*

The man responded, *"Yes."* I had seen him drop it. He didn't offer me a reward, after all, it was only $10. But God is my reward; righteous living is my reward. Holiness and pleasing the Father, those are my rewards. How much greater was I blessed for being honest than a liar or a thief?

> The desire of a man is his kindness, and a poor man
> is better than a liar. (Proverbs 19:22)

God is my Provider, not the devil. And now, having passed these tests, God has blessed me richly in finances and spiritual blessings.

God told the victors at Ai to destroy all the confiscated property, yet they bought some of the spoils out, claiming they were to sacrifice to God. God did not approve. He was not going to receive the sacrifice from accursed items then, and He doesn't do it now.

> But the children of Israel committed a trespass in the
> accursed thing for Achan... of the tribe of Judah took
> of the accursed thing. And the anger of the Lord was
> kindled against the children of Israel. (Joshua 7:1)

The *accursed* thing is anything that is set aside for God's use, or anything that is stolen or condemned. Anything that is not accepted by God, such as stolen goods, are cursed. If what you are offering God is spoils, that's a different story. The spoils are everything of value taken in battle, and because the Lord gives you victory, some of it is supposed to be dedicated to Him. Do not confuse the spoils that are to be dedicated or kept with *accursed* things.

The Tithing Relationship

Then the tithing tests. *Why so many tests?* That's how you get promotions. We all want promotions in the natural and spiritual. God knows what you're going to do in a certain situation. But do *you* know?

How much do you trust God, for instance? Enough to offer your first-born son? Thank God He's not asking that of us. Enough to give your best cow? OK, so we don't have any cows or goats. So do you trust Him enough to give your best and your very best? Not dress your best, but *give* your best. So your suit costs $400 and you gave God $5. Who are you worshipping? Self? Clothes? Others? I'm not saying don't look nice. I'm saying God first, then He'll give you an even better job, better than you think you have now. That includes better outfits, better health, better houses, better jobs, exceeding and abundantly over what you could ever ask or think.

Do you really *want* to tithe? Can God trust you with the tithe of 10. dollars on $100? Can He trust you with more? Can He promote you? You may be saying yes with your mouth, but what do your actions say? Can He bless you, now? He continues to test you in order to find out.

God First

I decided from the very beginning, not to struggle with the tithe. I decided how much I would like to tithe first, not how much I would like to *earn*. Then, God provided that and exceedingly and abundantly more than that. I had no trouble living on the 90%. God will make sure you won't have a problem living on nine times what you tithe. Even sinners can give 10% of their salary. Most do since it's tax deductible, but they don't give it to a church, necessarily. There are good causes set up in the world to circumvent that 10% from coming into the Church. When people realize they should give, they do. The world has set up middlemen to receive that 10%.

Charities are human causes, flesh and immediate. God's Church is the spiritual cause, spiritual and eternal. There is a vast difference. When people are properly taught to give, they bring the 10% to honor God to the House of God. God sets the order of paying tithes first, then offerings, finally alms, which is charity, giving to those less fortunate than oneself. I've always been thankful to God that I have a spiritual place to pay my tithes and give offerings: my church. It's part of my act of praise and worship.

In money worship equals the offering.

The Offering

Now we're ready to talk about the third level of experiencing God. When we experience God in the Spirit by our spirit, we worship Him. We have passed Thanksgiving, we have transcended Praise and moved into worship. As heirs, the gift in Thanksgiving, is the Tithe. In Praise and Worship, the Offering is the gift. The offering is something you aren't forced or required to give. You give it because of love, devotion and dedication. And when there is worship, it is as though God Himself comes down to accept that gift of worship from His precious saints and then He leaves or sends a blessing. (A receipt as it were.)

What is that blessing that He leaves? It's what you previously asked for. It's what you need. It's what is His good pleasure because He takes pleasure in the prosperity of his servant, (Psalm 25:37).

Worship is when we adore God for who He is. We love Him because He is God. We worship Him for His many attributes and Sovereignty. In worship we are not asking for anything. We are giving, and as we give, we activate the law of Sow and Reap. We sow in worship, and He gives back to us. We reap blessings and benefits. We are in the presence of God to love on Him, and we are in His presence to bless Him with the gift of adoration and the love offering, not for what He has already done for us, not because we want something from Him, but just because we love Him.

The offering is the gift. If there's no offering, there's no worship.

We wise men and women worship.

Three wise men did not come to offer Thanksgiving. They did not come to offer praise. They came to **worship** the King of kings. This Jesus had done nothing for them, so it wasn't Thanksgiving. And He hadn't yet done anything for anyone else they knew, so they didn't come to praise Him.

They came to worship Him.

You can be a wise man too. When you're getting dressed for church, you can flow into Thanksgiving, play and/or sing praise music on the way to church, move into praise. By the time you reach the sanctuary, you should already be ready to enter into worship.

By the time the wise men came from afar, they had moved from Thanksgiving, thankful that God had chosen them to praise, praising God for seeing the star, and ready to worship the newborn King. Like you, coming out of the world, coming out of sin--, they came from so far, they *had* to worship when they got there.

The wise men came with gifts--, pricey, costly, meaningful gifts to worship the child. How difficult that must have been to be honored and well known, wise men, and come to worship a *child*. These men must have had revelation. No one else was worshipping. Jesus save the shepherds and the angelic host. Angelic notice of His birth, and Anna and Simeon, by divine revelation, knew that the Christ child was born.

Herod knew, or suspected, and in his paranoia wanted to kill the child. But generally, folks in His town weren't worshipping Jesus. If they had, later in His life, Jesus would have been able to do great works in Nazareth. So, I'm saying that you must choose and will to worship God. It doesn't just "happen."

High Blessings

The Wise Men came to worship Jesus, and in return for their worship, they received what I call high blessings. What did they get? Stuff way above what you could think or imagine. Great wealth, miracles, prosperity, health, life, reputation, favor and honor.

And being warned of God in a dream that they should not return to Herod, they departed into their own country another way. Matthew 2:12

Because of their acts of worship, the three wise men were given more Wisdom than they already had, better wisdom--, divine Wisdom. In a dream, God spoke to them and gave them the information they needed not only to save their own lives, but the life of the Christ child. Because of worship, God was able to trust them with revelation, information, wealth and riches. And their ministry is a memorial forever. *Would you like to be in such a position?* Then worship the Lord. Worship Him with all your mind, body, soul--, with all your being. Worship Him in and out of the assembly. Worship Him with what is dear to you.

Worship him with the words of your mouth and out of your good treasure. We do not worship God for gain, but He is faithful to reward with high blessings.

Take a moment to reflect on Abraham's worship to God. He gave a tenth of all to Melchizedek; that was the tithe. Abraham's act of worship was the willingness and obedience to give Isaac, his only begotten, a child of promise. And if that is the case, then an awesome God has loved us enough, adorned us enough to give us His Only Begotten.

As you recall, God stopped Abraham from performing the actual sacrifice. Yeah, God did not stop Jesus on the Cross. That's love. But how many of us would be willing to part with things that we really love or want in order to *worship* God? How many are willing to be inconvenienced and really worship the Lord? How many of us would give a car or house or even our best suit of clothes? Not to mention the things that are truly dear to us. Of course I'm not suggesting Abraham's sacrifice, but are you willing to give up some relationships? (God wants to know, not me.) How many of us are willing to part with ungodly relationships as an act of respect, honor, praise, or even *worship* to the Lord? Sometimes giving up a relationship doesn't mean giving up the person, but sometimes it does.

Abraham had also given up relationships to obey God. He had given up Ishmael, and Hagar, but of great importance is that he was willing to sacrifice a relationship as an act of worship.

Further, God would not have asked Abraham for an offering if Abraham had not been obedient to tithe in the first place. If Abraham had not have tithed previously, Isaac would have been the tithe. A ram may not have been in that bush since the tithe is paid and the offering is given. Do you understand? Take a lesson: if we pay when and what God says pay, then we have the luxury of giving what we want to give later instead of having it taken away.

We want God's best in our lives. We want the anointing in our lives. The offering is the gift of the *kingly anointing*, the anointing that Abraham had. We want power, which is part of the kingly anointing. It's the anointing that causes people to move and things to happen when we speak. We want Mercy and Grace. We want to move in that next level, since we want all of that and so much more from God, so our offerings have to be pleasing to Him.

An offering is anything above and beyond the tithe. Always give something that is befitting a king. Give something that you value. Give something that you would want to receive. How do you know God is how you'll worship Him. You know him as the baby Jesus, you'll bring him a rattle, the noise of the air offering or clanging change. If you don't bring God, something fit for a king, then you don't know him as King, and He will not manifest Himself to you as King until you believe, (John 14:21).

I need to know Him as king. The Bible says that if you receive a profit in the name of a prophet, you will receive a prophet's reward. The same goes for the King. If you receive a king in the name of a king, you'll receive a King's reward. The wise men received Jesus as King, as the King of Glory, (Psalm 24). He is mighty in fighting my battles. I need to know Him as Sa'ba'oth, King of *kings*, which promotes me to royalty. I need to know Him as King so every knee of things in Earth and Heaven and under the Earth will bow to Him. I need to know Him as King because He took captivity captive and gave gifts to men.

He also gave us the keys of Heaven, which is binding and loosing, (Matthew 18:18). I need Him to manifest to me as King. Therefore I worship Him as a King because He is worthy.

How we worship God is reflected in the gifts, the offerings we give. Even in our daily lives, what we think of people is reflected in how we treat them. Think of your home life. Your air offering as the parent is just *being there*, bossing your wife and kids around, or the positive, telling them that you love them. It's important to tell others how you feel about them and that you love them, care about and appreciate them. But they say talk is cheap and to put your money where your mouth is—even in the world.

Think of the tithe as the basics and the offering as the topping on the cake. Think of the tithe as your house payment, utility bills, and food. Then think of the offering as your vacation or Caribbean cruise. If you gave your children a house to live in, food to eat and pay the utilities, that's the tithe, your reasonable service. They'd appreciate it, probably not getting too excited. The pride of a father who may or may not have grown up poor may rise when he's able to buy a new bedroom set for his seven-year-old son. That will not flow over as joy to the child; the boy is probably saying, *"Show me the toys."* And if you gave the child the offering of toys, how much more love would that child show their dad? Praise or even worship of the earthly sort is what you'll get for giving those gifts to a kid.

Breakfast in bed, for example, is a high blessing for Dad on Father's Day, or his birthday. That's quite an honor. Likewise, how can we get excited about His tithe? It's already God's; it belongs to Him. It is your reasonable service to pay it back, but the offering will excite God and move His hand to the 30, 60 and 100-fold return. ***High blessings***.

Do you remember these *high blessings*?

- Daniel gave devotedly of his time, energy, love and effort, sacrificing his flesh, and God gave him divine revelation. Dream, interpretation spared his life and gave him promotion.
- Mary, the mother of Jesus, gave selflessly of her reputation, and in faith conceived of the Holy Spirit, God blessed her to be the mother of Jesus.
- The widow woman at Zarephath put the man of God first, not the mall; God sustained her and her son through 3.5 famine years.
- Abraham received the high blessings of being the Father of Faith and the Father of Many Nations.

There are so many instances of God-given high blessings in the Bible and in our day. Don't be caught giving an *air offering*, just a dry wave to God, when you can at least tithe and at most pay your tithes and offerings. *Don't Refuse Me, Lord.* Then don't refuse to tithe. Then don't refuse the offering. Don't refuse to worship the King of kings.

Exercise:

High blessings I have received from God.

Count your high blessings.

www.King

We learned from the previous chapter that wise men worship the King and wise women worship the king. It's in the worship. The worship *is* the relationship.

The Catchers

God showed me the catchers in a vision. When children run out in the rain, they extend their arms and hands trying to catch rain drops. Or in winter they reach for snowflakes that float from the sky.

God showers blessings from Heaven. You may be one who sits or stands at your pew as the dew from Heaven is falling, but you're not trying to catch it. Where's the Wisdom in that? You'd put out a bucket to try to catch rainwater if you didn't have a well or running water with a tap faucet, wouldn't you? God is raining down blessings and that's a good thing because you need blessings. Why aren't you trying to catch them? Anointing is falling, if not because of you, at least you're in the midst of worshippers. It's an opportunity to *glean* some anointing. Even Eleanor Rigby knew to pick up the rice in the church where the wedding had been. God is raining down manna for those who are not well developed in faith. He's showering down blessings for those with a need, and anointing for those with faith and will do His will. Aren't you trying to catch any of it? The sane man is.

Perhaps God is not refusing you. Is He sending blessings that you need, blessings that you're not reaching out to receive? Maybe it's you who's refusing *Him*, not the other way around.

If you told your child that you would share your M & M's, what would that child do? Hold out his hands? If you open the bag and tilt it to pour out the colored candies, but your child doesn't cup his hands to receive? Of course not. You will refrain from pouring until the child holds out his hands to receive those colorful candy buttons. God also does not waste. If you believe God is pouring out blessings and showering, anointing, then aren't you a *catcher*? Aren't you in receive-mode, holding up holy hands? If not, He won't pour in your direction. If no one in the house is in receive-mode, the fresh anointing may just pass by. Remember the hymn, *Pass Me Not?* Then worship the Lord if you want Him to pour. He will not pour it out on the ground.

It's in the worship, but is the worship *in* you?

How can you worship when it's not in you? Whatever is in you will come out. When you're under pressure, God helps. If you're an orange, under pressure, orange juice will come out. If you have a foul mouth, under pressure, cuss words will come out. Life helps to see to that. But if you are a pray-er, when under pressure, prayers will come out. If you are a singer under pressure songs will come out. If you are worshipper, under pressure worship will come out.

You're in a situation where you really need God. You're under pressure to pay the bills, or get a job, or get over the pain you feel from an infirmity that's plaguing your body. You're under the pressure of a date with the surgeon's scalpel, which is scheduled for next week. You want to tell that surgeon, *"No, but I thank you very much."* That is some real pressure. The situation squeezes …and look what comes out. That's who you are.

Time goes by, the pressure increases. Now look what comes out. If you didn't know who you were before, you certainly know now. If prayers are in you, then God will hear you. If it's praise, then God will be encouraged. If it's worship, then God will be moved in your situation, God inhabits the praises of His people, and He will not refuse worship petitions and needs.

Get the devil out of you. In the worship service are those arms that should be outreached up toward God in worship, hanging limp and lifelessly by your side? If you're not in receive mode, you are in repel or I-don't-care mode. Are you even *standing* for that matter? Are you upset, and pouting because of not having it your way? You feel that church is lasting too long. Are you hostile? Is that what's in you? Hostility? Are people standing too close to you? Your pew neighbor touched you when they were lifting up holy hands and that offended you. Are your hands pushing your neighbor away from you or are they outstretched to the Heavens? When you selfishly push your neighbor away, you are misusing your hands. They could be uplifted to God to worship God.

With your attitude, or even physically, you may be trying to push the person off the place where they are to meet with the awesome presence of God, in so doing, you are pushing away your own blessings. How we treat our neighbor is looked upon by God.

How can you get worship in you?

Worship is always in you. We're all made to worship. We will worship *something--,* idol, sports figures, food, TV, money. It is in US, naturally. But you can get your worship on by studying to show your self approved and practicing the presence of God. Get to know Him, then you can worship Him. You can't possibly have a relationship with someone whom you don't know. All the blessings you know about and think about and want are in worship. He reveals Himself and you learn more and more about Him in worship. **High blessings** are worship. God will not refuse a worshipper.

www.king

The above heading is not a website address. It is the word the Lord gave. Wise women worship the king or why we wise men worship the king. It is not a dot com or a dot org. He is the king. So it's no doubt, but it could be a web address with God as the Webmaster www.king.god.

www.king

We wise men and wise women worship the king.

Crumbs in the Open

Now, church, I've come to tell you a little story.

I've come to tell the story of Hansel and Gretel.

They were walking along to Grandma's house one
day.

And as they walked along, trying to reach dear
Grandma.

They dropped crumbs along the way.

And as they dropped those crumbs.

Some birds flew right behind those two

and ate those breadcrumbs up.

When it was late and getting dark

They were lost and needed to find their way.

They needed to find their way back

but the night was black.

It was night and they were in the woods and

Needed to find their way back home.

But they had a problem.

They couldn't find their way.

They couldn't find the direction home.

Now Hansel and Gretel couldn't find their way home.

Because they didn't acknowledge God to direct their paths. They didn't acknowledge God and they didn't **plant** their seed.

They didn't acknowledge God because they didn't plant their seed.

They sowed. Yes, they sowed a little, but they didn't **plant** in Jesus.

That day, they dropped the little on the way just past Sister Sally's house.

They dropped a little on the way as they passed Brother Sammy's house.

They dropped a little on the way as they passed their neighbor's house.

They dropped a little on the way as they passed their cousin's house.

And he said, *"Sally, which way to Grandma's?"*

She said, Brother Sammy, *"Which way to Grandmas?"*

"Neighbor Man, were going to Grandma's."

Even Cousin pointed the way to Grandma's.

But they had a problem. They couldn't find Grandma's,

Because they hadn't acknowledged God to direct their paths.

They haven't acknowledged God in their sowing.

And they hadn't **planted** in the Lord.

Now they were lost and all they could think about was going back home.

But Hansel and Gretel had a problem.

And the problem was they didn't **plant** any seed.

They had laid their seed out in the open at Sister Sally's house.

They left their seed out in the open at Brother Sammy's house.

They cast their seed out in the open as they passed by their neighbor's house. And,

They dropped that seed as they passed their cousin's house.

But now, they had a problem.

They thought because of that seed, they could go back when they had a need. To Sister Sally, to Brother Sammy, to their neighbor.

Or to their cousin.

But they couldn't go back the way they came.

They thought when they had a need, they could depend on people.

They thought when they had a need, they could ask the people they had helped when they were prosperous.

But like the song says, you may never pass this way again.

Most folks will tell you to change those words to,

Please don't ever pass this way again, especially if you need money.

Hansel and Gretel thought that with all the crumbs they had sowed, they could reap again when they needed help.

But those people--, from Sally to Sammy to their

Neighbor and Cousin had eaten those crumbs, those seeds.

Because they were not **planted** in the Lord, they could not go back to those who had received

the crumbs and receive back from them again.

They had a problem because they had not **planted** in the Lord. They had a problem because they had used only crumbs.

They had a problem because they had sown to the folks they knew.

And had not *sown* or **planted** in the Lord.

They had a problem because Jesus is the only one who can **multiply**. Your relatives don't know divine math. They just *divided* what you gave them among themselves or added it to their bank accounts. And subtracted it out when they went to the mall.

Hansel and Gretel had a problem because those birds, Sister Sally. Brother Sammy, neighbor man and Cousin had eaten all those crumbs. Like the little birds, they ate those crumbs. And in the aftermath, there was none.

Jesus is the only one who can divinely multiply. They had a problem because they had not planted in the Lord. They hadn't hid that gift in Jesus, but they sowed it in the open for all to see. They sowed it so all could be impressed with what they had to give. Jesus is the only one who can divinely multiply.

By God's Grace, when it's time to plant your seed, plant it in the Lord, so when you need direction, when you need to find your way. When it's late in the midnight hour, when it's dark, when the path is dim. You've acknowledged Him already and He will direct your path.

God wants to know, where have you been?

Acknowledge God, He'll bring you back in.

. Where have you been?

He'll direct your path.

And bring you back in.

If you find that you're out someplace where you did not want to be or plan to be, then God is telling you to acknowledge Him. God is asking you to acknowledge Him because you did it your way, not His way.

You were prosperous, you were successful, and you had everything you needed, and now for some reason, you may have experienced a financial reversal because you have not been doing the things that you should have been doing. You had it made, you didn't tithe, you didn't give offerings, you didn't do anything in the Household of Faith. Can you say that you've been to church at least half the Sundays in a year? But you're certainly calling on God now for a financial windfall, for favor in a job interview. You're calling on God, and it seems like He's refusing you. You want God to fix it.

God is not the back up plan, God is THE PLAN.

When you had prosperity, you spent all your time and money on other people, friends and family members. Trying to impress them and you did impress them. But one thing about impressions is that they fade over time. Press your finger into your arm for about 30 seconds, see how it leaves an impression. Wait a minute, then look at it. It's this, though your finger never impressed your arm at all. Family and friends are that way, especially about gifts, treats, and trinkets.

They will boldly ask you, *What will you bring me next time? What you gave me last time is already used up or broken. Impress me again. Just keep impressing me.* False friends and users will use you up, but I guess you already know that because you were calling on God to reverse your reversal of fortune.

Those were crumbs, and you were sowing to impress. They were only crumbs, although it may have seemed like you were a high roller. Maybe in your neighborhood, in your neck of the woods, you were Mr. Big. But those bucks you were throwing around were only crumbs to Sally, Sammy, your neighbor and your cousin, but God could have used that money to bless you mightily. God knows Divine Math. He would have blessed you, with prosperity, direction, guidance, and with other spiritual blessings.

So when you're in that high place, who are you blessing? God or your friends and family--, your *skin-folks*? Yes, the Bible says to love one another. But **after** you bless God, not instead of. These are some of the mistakes that people make, spiritually. When you tie God's hands, He must say, "No."

Thank God we now know better.

Our God is full of Mercy. It's not too late; if you acknowledge Him, He won't refuse you. He will take you back in.

Exercise:

Have I acknowledged God fully in my life?

Starting today, I will acknowledge God in these three areas:

1.

2.

3.

Change

I can think of many kinds of change, three of which are.

1. The kind you receive after a purchase.
2. Two tens for $20, so each child can have allowance.
3. God's kind. 30, 60, 100-fold return. This is the best kind.

Change is good, but unless you made less than $10 this week, not in the offering plate. We talk about money because it's something that we all understand and need, just to exist. Money is something that people seek, sometimes lusting for it to their own demise. And as we continue to petition God for *things and stuff*, He speaks back to us about **change**. God is concerned about your character and your well-being. He tells us in His Word about the lust of money, prosperity, and the principles of sowing and reaping. He teaches us how to give and receive. He gives us power to get wealth and rebukes the Devourer so we can enjoy our wealth.

And God speaks to us about the power of change. Some of us want so much from God, but for our own good and His divine Wisdom and Mercy, He keeps things from us and us from things that would hurt us. Sometimes that thing is *money*. God does not want to keep us in perpetual poverty, but He wants us prepared to receive and remain blessed after He showers prosperity upon us. God sometimes is requesting that we change.

We see ourselves in the Word; we see what we *should* be. We hear sermons, read books such as this one, and receive prophetic words, and good counsel, all for the express purpose of growth, which definitely means **change**. God wants to bless us and prosper us, but He also requests that we be flexible and willing to be made and remade from glory to glory.

God is waiting for you to become the *you* that He's going to bless.

We expect God to change. *What?* The Scriptures say He changes not, that's true, but when we need Jehovah Rapha, the Lord our Healer, we may be disappointed when God shows up in the full glory of another of His attributes. If He's not the one we need, then we are not pleased. We expect God to change, in a sense, to know what we need, when we need it, and to be at our beck and call.

But we also change, and we must change. Sometimes we are great intercessory warriors, sometimes we are prophetic speakers, sometimes we are ministers of comfort or healing. As we expect of God, we must change for the situation, and we *can* change. At work we are administrators, secretaries or managers, while at home we are mommies and daddies. Then at church we are praise leaders, sopranos or tenors in the choir, and ushers. As long as we are going through the process and the trouble or joy, of changing, why not change according to what God has planned for you to become? Why not follow the steps that the Lord has ordered for you and your life? You're going to change anyway, physically, hopefully, intellectually, emotionally and spiritually. Why not to the glory of God, and for the best?

Whatever we are asking God for, He wants to give it, but He is just waiting for you to become the *you* that He will bless. And He will not bless halfway, but fully and abundantly.

Has God placed prophetic cashiers at McDonald's, Walmart, and gas stations? They keep handing us nickels, dimes, quarters, and pennies – is God trying to tell us something? **Change**. Change the way we think about, handle and feel about money. Change the way you use money. Change yourself and then He can change the amount and the flow of money and abundance around you. Change to be the way you know you're supposed to be about giving and blessing God, the man of God, in the House of God, and then God will trust you to be a channel of blessing.

People can change if _they_ want to, but the only human that's changeable is a baby, its diaper, and many times that with a struggle.

Change an adult's character or nature? We've probably all tried it, or at least wished it. It's not possible, but people can change if _they_ choose. Truly, the only real and lasting change must come by the Cross.

Don't Refuse Me, Lord. So it is our responsibility to change, to move from glory to glory and from faith to faith, as God perfects that which concerns us.

> The Lord will perfect that which concerns me. Thy mercy, O Lord, endureth forever. Forsake not the works of thine own hands. Psalms 138: 8

I prayed the above Scripture for years. I was wanting, waiting for God to fix everybody that irked _me_ and to fix all those people who, in my eyes, did really stupid things. Well, He fixed them alright, as He *perfects the things that concerned me*, not the people that I knew, not those things that concerned other people, but the things that concerned **me**. If someone is getting on my nerves, they can change, or I can change the way I respond or react to them if I'm spiritually sensitive. I may realize that the reason they're acting that way is because spiritually they are not where they should be, or they might just be having a bad day, (often the case), or they don't know any better. I might realize that I am put in their company to model proper Christian behavior to them and possibly learn something from them. Often, I believe that my being around the unsaved is to plant a seed, or *water* until God gives the increase. And if they irk me, it's just their flesh getting on my *highly developed spiritual nerves*. I should not be bothered by their not being saved or being ignorant of God and holiness, other than caring about their eternal soul.

Still know that when you are walking upright before the Lord, and you stay prayed up --, demons will manifest. (Wow, I had a lot to learn!)

When I'm around professed Christians who hurt me, well, let's say that really helps *my* prayer life.

The reason we can see the things that other people are doing that are wrong or stupid is because we don't have temptation in that area. We may have overcome temptation in that area that we see, it means that we can avoid it--, thank God. Most sin happens by deception. Those things we don't see are the stupid things _**we**_ do. Those are the things that help other people's prayer lives, if they are praying to God on our behalf, instead of gossiping about us or arguing with us. He shows us ourselves, then corrects us if we yield to His correction. That's what the correction is all about. God is making you over daily. He is making you into the _**you**_ that He's going to bless.

Don't Refuse Me, Lord. Then don't refuse the correction that leads to perfection.

Change may take a while, but you can.

Change.

Dear Reader

Thank you for purchasing this volume, we pray for your complete victory and success in life, in the Name of Jesus.

Amen.

Author, Dr. Marlene Miles

Enjoy Bible teaching and messages on the Dr. Miles YouTube Channel.

Find spiritual warfare prayers on the Warfare Prayer Channel on YouTube.

Christian books by this author

AK: Adventures of the Agape Kid

AMONG SOME THIEVES

As My Soul Prospers

Behave

Churchzilla (The Wanna-Be Bride of Christ)

The Coco-So-So Correct Show

Demons Hate Questions

Devil Weapons: *Anger, Unforgiveness & Bitterness*

Do Not Orphan Your Seed

Do Not Work for Money

Don't Refuse Me Lord

The FAT Demons

got Money?

Let Me Have a Dollar's Worth

Living for the NOW of God

Lord, Help My Debt

Lose My Location

Made Perfect In Love

The Man Safari *(Really, I'm Just Looking)*

Marriage Ed., *Rules of Engagement & Marriage*

The Motherboard: *Key to Soul Prosperity*

Name Your Seed

Plantation Souls

The Poor Attitudes of Money

Power Money: Nine Times the Tithe

The Power of Wealth

Seasons of Grief

Seasons of War

SOULS in Captivity

Soul Prosperity: Your Health & Your Wealth

The *spirit* of Poverty

The Throne of Grace, *Courtroom Prayers*

Time Is of the Essence

Triangular Powers (4 book series)

Warfare Prayer Against Poverty

When the Devourer is Rebuked

The Wilderness Romance

<u>Other Journals & Devotionals by this author</u>:

The Cool of the Day – Journal

got HEALING? Verses for Life

got HOPE? Verses for Life

got GRACE? Verses for Life

got JOY? Verses for Life

got PEACE? Verses for Life

got LOVE? Verses for Life

He Hears Us, Prayer Journal *4 colors*

I Have A Star, Dream Journal *kids, teen, adult*

I Have A Star, Guided Prayer Journal,

J'ai une Etoile, Journal des Reves

Let Her Dream, Dream Journal

Men Shall Dream, Dream Journal,

My Favorite Prayers (in 4 styles)

My Sowing Journal (in three different colors)

Tengo una Estrella, Diario de Sueños

Illustrated children's books by this author:

Big Dog (8-book series)

Do Not Say That to Me

Every Apple

Fluff the Clouds

I Love You All Over the World

Imma Dance

The Jump Rope

Kiss the Sun

The Masked Man

Not During a Pandemic

Push the Wind

Tangled Taffy

What If?

Wiggle, Wiggle; Giggle, Giggle

Worry About Yourself

You Did Not Say Goodbye to Me

Notes:

www.ingramcontent.com/pod-product-compliance
Lightning Source LLC
Chambersburg PA
CBHW060022050426
42448CB00012B/2845